You Are My Son

You Are My Son

A Mother's Journey On Raising An Autistic Child

PATRICIA DEGEYTER

AuthorHouse™ LLC
1663 Liberty Drive
Bloomington, IN 47403
www.authorhouse.com
Phone: 1-800-839-8640

Published by AuthorHouse 07/29/2013

ISBN: 978-1-4817-7918-0 (sc)
ISBN: 978-1-4817-7919-7 (hc)
ISBN: 978-1-4817-7920-3 (e)

Library of Congress Control Number: 2013913258

Contents

Acknowledgment

I would like to take a moment here to recognize the best mother in the world in my eyes—my mother, Josephine Powell. My dear mother is always showing extreme love for all her family. She has showed me so much love and devotion in the hardest, most difficult time in my life. While supporting me, listening to me without hesitation, speaking to me with such loving compassion, and never criticizing me on my faults, she guided me to be the best mother I could possibly be. I will always and forever be so very grateful to her. She helped me more than I think she realizes. She has shown so much love, devotion, care, and deep concern for my special child. My mother is always there for us, as she has always been. My son is the luckiest boy to have such a wonderful, lovely, compassionate grandmother. Thank you Mom, I love you so much!

I would also like to recognize a very special man in my life, my loving and handsome father, Gaylord "Buzz" Powell. My father loved my son very much and was very instrumental in helping my son achieve his ability in many areas. My father would help Matthew to work on the computer and allowed my son to use his own personal computer with no fear, knowing Matthew knew what to do. He also introduced my son to start therapeutic horseback riding. He would take my son for long walks down the river and they would enjoy throwing rocks in the water, while my father talked with my son to teach him all he could. My father has since passed away. How I miss and love him dearly. I wish my story could have been done before his passing. My son is very lucky to have had a wonderful, loving, and caring grandfather, who was always proud of him and was always there for us, in our time of need. Thank you Dad, I love you and miss you so much!

Introduction

My name is Patricia DeGeyter. I am the mother of a very special child with autism. My son's name is Matthew. This is my story, which I am sharing to help other parents who have had the devastating diagnosis of autism for their special child and are in a similar situation to mine. My main goal is to help you in trying to cope and to let you know there is much hope for your autistic child. I know all the emotions you are feeling. The information in this book is intended to give you a more positive outlook toward the challenges that you and your special child will face in the future.

In my story, I will be taking you on a journey through my experiences raising an autistic child—good and bad. I will detail my struggles and accomplishments with and expectations for my son. I will recognize those who were most helpful to me during this difficult time in my life. I'll also call out the not-so-friendly individuals in the world who were rude and hurtful to my son and I.

Back when my son was first diagnosed with autism, the Internet was not a regular household commodity. The books out there at the time, particularly encouraging ones, were very scarce. I purchased a book that was recommended to me, and all it did was frighten me. It gave me no hope. In my opinion, it was definitely not the type of book parents of a child newly diagnosed with autism should be reading. It only focused on the negativity and heartache of the diagnosis.

I needed more of an optimistic and encouraging book. I needed a book to read that offered a parent's point of view on how to raise an autistic child, a book that would give me hope and not just despair. That's what I've tried to provide you with here—a look into my life raising a child with autism. You will see the possibility that your special child can learn and function in society.

These special children are very teachable and have many great hidden talents that are not always recognizable at first. As parents, we must work hard to find the great gifts our special children have. I hope to give you encouragement that—through diligence, love, patience, managing very difficult situations, and care—your child's formidable efforts will not be in vain. Children with autism are capable of doing many wonderful, great things. You can give your child the strength and self-confidence to accomplish and become a productive and independently successful person, a wonderful addition to our society.

I don't mean to convey that the road to adulthood will not include days of frustration, exhaustion, and anger among all those other emotions you may be feeling. However, today I see my son as a young adult, a true blessing in my life. Those who have not had the privilege or the opportunity to work with and know my son (who has turned out to be a wonderful and loving young man) have maybe not yet met a special autistic person who has overcome many obstacles. They would be amazed by him. I know in my heart that God has given me a very special child with a special purpose in life. All special-needs children, regardless of what their disability may be, are amazing individuals in my eyes.

I know there are parents out there in this world dealing with much more difficult situations with their children, and how I pray for them always. Whatever the situation we are enduring with our special children, they all matter and they all count. All these special-needs children must be honored, respected, and given much love and devotion.

Another reason I am writing this story about my life in raising my special son is to give you faith, from a parent's point of view, that there is much success and great hope in having a child with autism. Never, ever give up, in spite of whatever negativity others may send your way. Always stick up for your child. Never allow someone to be grossly misleading to you and your child. Hold on to your faith and be prepared to work very, very hard for your autistic child. Learn and know your legal rights—this is very important.

Never accept anything less than success for your child. Not to say there weren't times my husband and I wanted to just give up because we were so frustrated and exhausted, but we knew that would never, ever happen. I also think it is very important for parents to find a support group they can go to as an outlet.

With support groups, you may need to try a few before you find one that's the right fit. I remember one autism support group my husband and I went to where we were telling a story about something Matthew did that we thought was so wonderful, and one of the members of the group said, "What did your son do, leave his autism at home that day?" I could not believe that a parent of an autistic child would respond in that manner. We thought everyone would be happy for us and our child because they knew what it was like to deal with autism on a daily basis. Clearly, that was the wrong group for us.

I remember another autism support group I attended by myself. This group mainly consisted of mothers. A lot of autism support groups were that way at the time. One mother in particular spoke of how her own parents did not want anything to do with her autistic child. She said that her child was not even welcome at the grandparents' house. She continued on to say that her husband had abandoned her and their autistic child. We all were so saddened to hear her speak of this. The more she spoke, the more I cried in disbelief, and how my heart ached for her. I felt horrible for her. Everyone there did. Not a dry eye in the room.

I felt guilty about the situation she was in, because I had two sets of loving grandparents for my child, and they all showed much love toward him. How this woman ever got through that, I will never know. I prayed for her and her child, that things would get better in their lives. I tried to keep a journal about our lives dealing with autism because I thought maybe some of my information may help other parents that may have to deal with an autistic child themselves. However, this was much too difficult to accomplish, as autism took over my life and I could not find the time to keep up with it. All of my attention was now directed to my son. I always thought since my son was diagnosed with autism, I would possibly be able to provide some hope and encouragement with all of our experiences, but I was unable to keep that journal going. I always said to myself throughout the years dealing with autism, *I am going to write a book one day*. It took me quite a long time to go down memory lane. It was also very hard to remember everything we endured and it was saddening to go back to all those difficult years.

Remember to always listen to your heart and hold on tightly to your faith. God always listens and will help you get through it, with the power of many prayers.

Chapter 1

Early Years

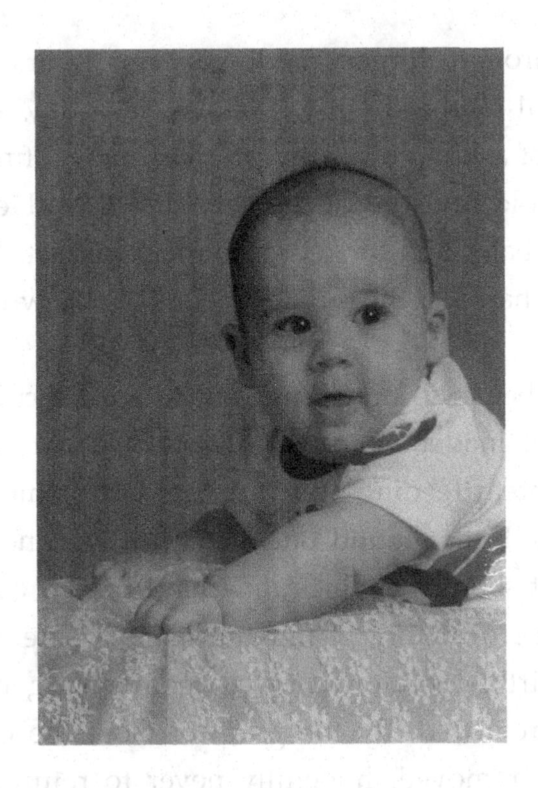

On March 21, 1992, the most precious little boy came into my life. Weighing in at eight pounds five ounces, he looked perfect. I was very fortunate to have my husband, Matt, and my mother in the delivery room with me. When I needed a stronger hand, I had my husband, and when I needed a more gentle hand, I had my loving mother.

At 10:20 p.m., after multiple hours of a very difficult labor and delivery, I had to be rushed to surgery because I was bleeding so excessively that the doctor was afraid I was starting to hemorrhage. That was the first time I felt like I was not a normal mother. I was so saddened that I could not hold my baby but was taken away from him instead.

I got through surgery and woke up hours later with my beautiful mother by my side. The next day, after hours and hours of asking to see my precious baby, I finally got to meet and hold my son for the very first time. He was such a beautiful baby and looked absolutely perfect. He had so much black hair and the most gorgeous big brown eyes.

When I began to nurse my son, I had difficulty with it. Again, I felt inadequate, like I was not a normal mother. I thought breastfeeding was supposed to come naturally, instinctively. I later found out that I had melanoma cancer on my right shoulder, which may have been a contributing factor for the difficulty in nursing on that side. Soon after my son's birth, I underwent yet another surgery to have the cancer removed. By the grace of God, the cancer was successfully removed, hopefully never to return. Still, my son would not nurse on that side at all afterward. Thankfully, I was able to breastfeed with my left breast.

Matthew was not a good sleeper at all. We were lucky if he slept for twenty minutes at a time. (It wasn't until he was four years old that he managed to stay asleep all night—and then I kept waking up because I felt I had to constantly check on him; it seemed like something was wrong for him to sleep so soundly!) My husband and I were both working full-time jobs, and we needed to find a way to get our son to sleep more to receive much-needed rest. We finally realized that Matthew would fall asleep if we took him for walks in the red wagon, so we decided to try that at bedtime.

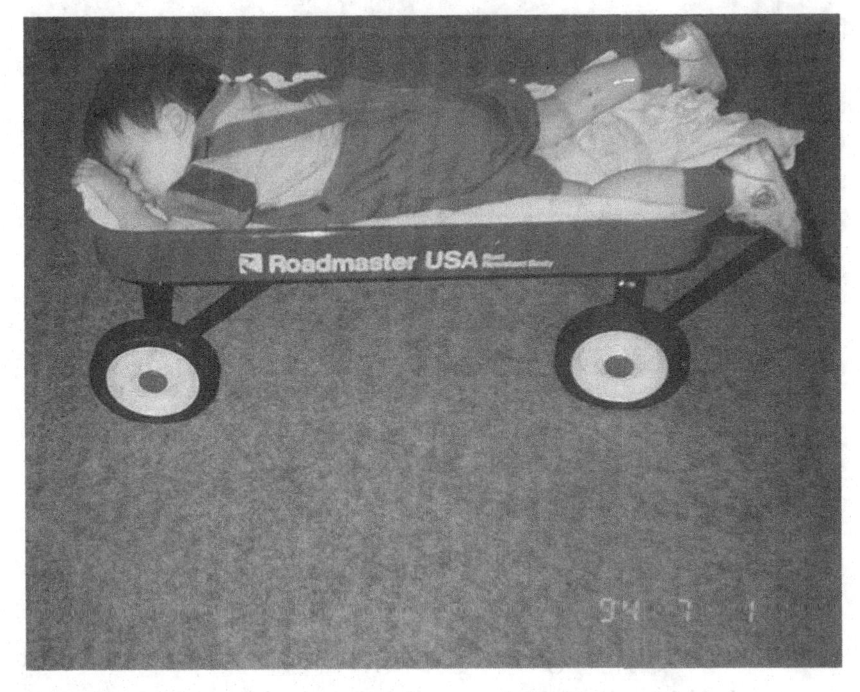

The wagon we used to put Matthew asleep

We thought if we brought the wagon indoors and made a bed out of it, lining it with blankets, it would comfort him. We needed to keep the wagon moving constantly, though, so we would sit there for hours upon hours in a rocking chair moving the wagon back and forth until he fell asleep. It finally worked, but the moment we would stop the momentum of the wagon, Matthew would instantly wake up and start screaming and crying. This went on for a few years, but finally one day he stayed asleep when we stopped the wagon. *A miracle!* we thought. We were shocked and happy that something finally worked.

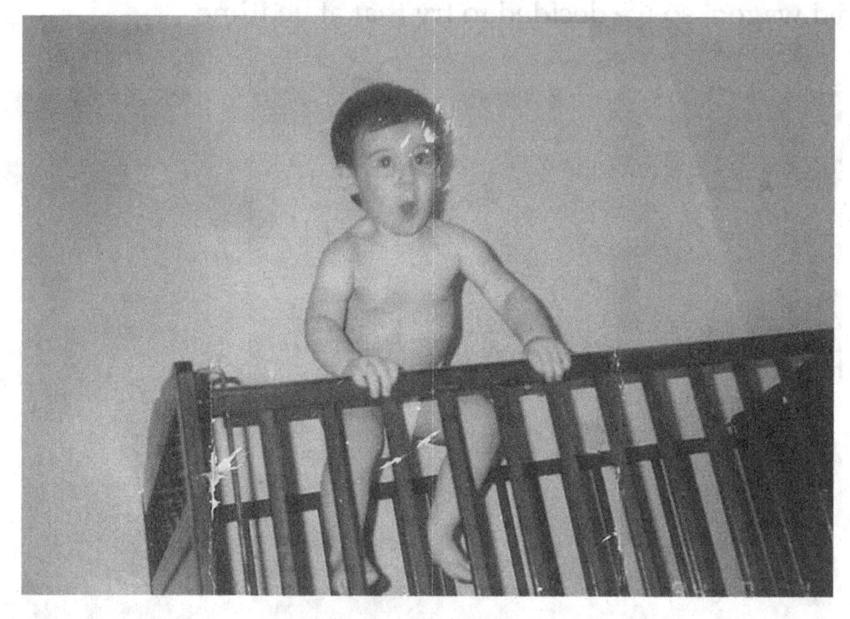

Our bouncing baby boy

He eventually outgrew the wagon and had no choice but to sleep in his crib. Matthew didn't mind it too much. He loved to hold on to the railing of the crib and bounce in it.

Whenever I did laundry, I would put Matthew in his crib before I ran downstairs to get the clothes. One day I put him in his crib, went downstairs, and came back up minutes later to find Matthew out of his crib. I knew I had put him in there and had no idea how he had gotten out. I was so mentally and physically exhausted that I was second-guessing myself. I put him in the crib again, walked out of the room, and acted like I was going downstairs. Matthew then started to jump in his crib, and after four great leaps he soared out of the crib and onto the floor. I was totally shocked—not only that he had jumped out of the crib, but that he had landed perfectly on his feet. There was no way I could leave him alone now. I had no safe place to put him, so he had to come with me everywhere I went.

I remember looking at myself in the mirror one day and seeing how tired I looked and how frustrated I was feeling. I said to myself, *I did not realize being a parent would be so difficult.* As I said this, of course, I was crying as I always seemed to be doing, all the time. I wondered how in the world my mother and my husband's mother managed to take care of so many children at one time.

Matthew seemed to be very unhappy all of the time. He was nonverbal and also had cognitive delays. I couldn't help but wonder if it was something I was doing wrong. I felt like such a horrible mother because I just could not make my baby happy; I couldn't even get a smile. It made my depression even worse. He never wanted to be held and would constantly push us away when we tried to hold him. It was like trying to hold onto a wet noodle slipping out of our grasp, with all of his mighty strength.

At this young age, our son had overwhelming power. I was a little over one hundred pounds, and I was no match for his strength. I still had all the stitches in my shoulder from the removal of my melanoma cancer, which caused me great pain when I had to struggle with Matthew.

I had a hard time comforting my little boy when he was upset or angry, which was most of the time. That broke my heart into pieces. Imagine your child rejecting you, day after day after day—and I really do mean *day after day after day*. I would see other mothers with their children, getting love and communication. I was so envious because I never got that, and I wanted it so badly. I craved it. I would have paid for it if had to. I wanted to know why I was not chosen, as a mother, to be worthy of that.

At this point, I started to get very, very angry—extremely angry. I remember being at the park with my son and seeing all of the children playing so well together, talking, interacting appropriately with each other and having fun . . . but there was my son, all by himself, preferring his solitary play. I tried to be with my son and interact with him, but he preferred to just sit there and be by himself. He would get horribly upset and cry if I tried to be with him. I felt everyone's eyes were on me, thinking, *What is she doing to that boy to upset him so greatly?* I would kiss my son on top of his head and walk back to where I was sitting and just sit there, watching him with a very close eye. Which was something, I always did anyways. I watched him like a hawk.

As I sat there watching, I could hear all the other parents having fun with their children, like normal families do. I would sit crying silently and put my hands up to my ears. I prayed so hard, asking God to please let me hear my son's voice and be with my child, like all the other parents were able to do. I didn't want to hear their children's voices—I wanted to hear *my* child's voice. I felt very, very guilty about that. When I would hear a parent tell her children to "be quiet," I would get so upset. I wanted to tell that mother how lucky she was that her children were communicating with her, even if the kids were complaining or asking for something.

When Matthew was thirteen months old, my son was severely burned by a hot cup of coffee I had mistakenly left on the dining-room table. I had turned my back for just a moment to rewind a cartoon tape he had been watching, which I knew was over because he was screaming and crying. In the few seconds that I had my back turned, he managed to pull the cup of coffee toward him, try to drink it, and pour it onto himself.

He was only wearing a diaper at the time. (This happened at the end of June, and we only had a small window air-conditioner to cool the whole house. He also preferred to wear just a diaper anyways.) I remember turning around in complete devastation; I could not believe what had just happened to my precious son. I immediately grabbed him and called 911. He was screaming in horrific agony. I was in pure shock and mortified, screaming and crying myself.

I had such a hard time speaking to the operator. They sent a police officer along with an ambulance to my home because of all of the distress. Skin was peeling off Matthew's precious little body. It felt like such a horrible nightmare.

Matthew was rushed to the hospital, where they had to put an IV into his head and put him in a crib with a plastic bubble around it. His injury was significant, starting at his mouth and trailing down to just above his pelvic region. He was burned over 40 percent of the front of his body. It haunts me to this day when I think about it. I hated myself severely. How could I have been so careless? Maybe I was so mentally and physically drained that I was just not thinking straight that day.

During the two weeks Matthew spent in the hospital before we were able to bring him home, many family members came to visit. My son wouldn't respond to many people, not even to his own parents. However, my mother was someone he would respond too. She and Matthew have a great connection, and my son really deeply loves her, as I do. Another person he responded to was his first cousin Stevie Charlie, my sister Mef's son. He came in one day, gently held on to Matthew's hand, and said, "Matthew, Stevie Charlie is here." Matthew's eyes lit up and he turned toward his cousin and smiled. To this day, my son has a strong connection with his cousin. He even chose Stevie to be his confirmation sponsor.

After Matthew came home from the hospital, I had to have a nurse come to the house every morning to help me change Matthew's bandage. We had to wrap him almost like a mummy to keep the burn wound from getting infected. I had to hold my son down with him screaming and crying in such pain while the nurse used tongue depressors to smear cream over the burned areas of his body. Again, I felt horrible, and having to watch this being done to my child was so heart-wrenching for me—not to mention what my dear child was going through. My precious son was in so much agony. I cannot express how I hated myself for letting this horrible accident happen. My heart was in such despair and ached so greatly for my special son.

After the accident, Matthew had to learn all over again how to sit and how to walk. When he was finally on the road to recovery, he still had no vocabulary, and we started to notice very odd behavior. He always preferred solitary play, lining up Matchbox cars on the windowsill. When he was outside, he liked to sit in a pile of small rocks; then, taking the rocks one by one, he would make a pile on one side of his body, and once that was complete, he would make a pile on the other side of his body. This could go on for hours.

This was pure enjoyment for him. However, what could be so fascinating to a child about piling up small rocks from one side of his body to the other side? We could not allow that to continue all the time, as we were constantly trying to teach him other things that were more appropriate for his age. But in his mind, we were just irritating him.

Another odd behavior: our son would like his father to throw a football up in the tree in our backyard so that he could watch it bounce off the branches of the tree coming down toward him. Matthew enjoyed this tremendously. I was very thankful that my son looked perfectly normal, although some of his odd behaviors (including hand-flapping when excited) brought too much unwanted attention toward us.

One day he was playing strangely by lining up his toy cars on the windowsill again and making sure they were all perfectly lined up in a row. It had to be perfect, and not one thing could be out of place. This is how it was with everything. If things weren't perfect, he would get extremely upset and scream and cry. Even a simple haircut was so challenging and detrimental to my son. I wanted to understand my son's world, but I also wanted to live as normally as possible and have him learn about our world.

I knew in my heart by this time that we were living in two totally different worlds. He never would respond to us when we called out his name. He just completely ignored us. This particular day as he lined up the cars, I went behind Matthew, and with my head at an angle away from his head, I screamed as loud as I could. He did not even flinch. At this point, my husband and I thought our son was possibly deaf.

We also thought that maybe the burn was so traumatic that it caused this behavior to happen. We were lost and confused once again.

At the time this happened, we lived near railroad tracks. One day when Matthew heard a train coming, he ran to the window to see it. My husband and I knew our son could not possibly be deaf, since he heard the train coming. So why was he not responding when we called out his name? We had his hearing checked just to make sure.

We were grateful that Matthew was not deaf and was able to hear. But what the hell was going on? Again, as usual, we were so very, very lost and confused. Another odd behavior we noticed with Matthew was that when he was in his crib, he would just start to laugh for no apparent reason. When we would go into his room, we saw nothing to stimulate his laughter, and yet he would be laughing. He would then just babble in his own language. We were so confused and so lost once again.

Another incident I remember is one day when I was cooking dinner, I let Matthew sit on the clean kitchen floor and play with some pots and pans. He was ignoring me as usual and playing in his own little world, although he was having so much fun. I reached to get something out of the cabinet, and I left the cabinet door open. All of a sudden, out of nowhere, Matthew went from a pleasant state of playing to crying and screaming. I was shocked at the sudden change. I reached for him and searched around frantically to see what was upsetting him. I could not understand what had caused his distress. What was going on? He was happy moments ago banging on pots and pans, having so much fun. Why all of a sudden the change in behavior? I tried everything to calm him down, but nothing worked.

Emotionally frustrated by his behavior, I finally set him gently back on the floor and slammed that cabinet door shut in pure frustration. I was so surprised and shocked to find that he instantly stopped crying and continued to play and be happy. I literally fell to my knees in extreme confusion with tears flowing down my face. I just couldn't comprehend how a simple cabinet door being left open could mean that much to a child. (Today I understand why—because having the cabinet door open was out of sequence.)

At this point, we were extremely tired and worried about our son. Our families tried to help us as much as they could, but they all had full-time jobs and children of their own to take care of. Our parents always watched Matthew for us if our schedules conflicted sometimes, as I had to work day shifts instead of mainly nights. Our families were always there for us and helped us as much as possible. We will always be so grateful to all of them for their love and support.

Matt would work days and I would work nights. As soon as Matt got home from work, he would take over caring for

Matthew, and I know how hard that must have been. One day he must have been extremely tired, because Matt fell asleep, and our son turned on the faucet and let the sink fill up. Thank God he used only cold water. Matt said that when he woke up and heard Matthew in the bathroom, our boy was having such fun with such joy splashing a washcloth all around with water coming over the edge of the basin. Needless to say, the bathroom was flooded; it ended up warping the floor, which we then had to replace.

After yet another day of being so exhausted, I was alone with Matthew—Matt was working, and I had no one to watch our son so I could get some much-needed rest. I put Matthew in his crib. I locked the bathroom door so he couldn't get in. Then I laid on the floor in front of his bedroom door so he couldn't get out. I thought I had covered all of my bases, making sure there was nothing in Matthew's room that he could harm himself with, and I fell into an exhausted slumber.

I slept for about an hour and a half, and when I woke up, I found his room full of feces. It was everywhere. All over the walls, floor, just everywhere. He used it as if it was chalk. I was so angry. All I had wanted at that time was a little rest. Again, I cried and cried, looked at my special child, and said, "Mom has a lot of cleanup work to do, doesn't she? First, let's get you a bath." He again babbled in his own language to me. I had to get this mess cleaned up before I started my work night, and before my husband returned home from his work day.

I remember another incident that happened around the time Matthew was two years old. As usual, he was having a very bad day. He was screaming and crying, and there was nothing I could do to calm him down. Finally, I got so frustrated, I walked past him and, as I did this, I swept the silk chiffon robe that I was wearing over his body. He started laughing and smiling. I was elated to hear the sounds of joyfulness in his laughter. I was amazed, so from that point on, I would stand for hours twirling my robe as he ran through it. I was getting so tired, but if it meant I got to hear my son laugh and see his smiling face, I didn't care how bad my arms hurt. I just wanted to see my precious son happy. It was a wonderful experience to see happiness in my son and to hear his laughter. So I would continue to twirl that robe until he wanted to stop. Some days it worked wonderfully, and other days he wanted nothing to do with it.

At this point in his life, my son had little to no vocabulary. This was such a concern for us. Matthew had no voice until he was four years old. His first word ever spoken was *tolekay* (tool-a-kay). I asked him what that was, and he had no response for me. I sat there and thought, *What the hell is a tolekay?* I looked over at my son and asked him again, "What is a tolekay?" and in amazement he answered me, "No see, no tolekay." I replied, "Well, if you no see no tolekay, I certainly don't see no tolekay."

Out of curiosity and most importantly wanting to know what this meant, I looked it up in the dictionary the best I could, and there was no such word to be found. I wasn't even sure I knew how to spell it. But it meant the world to me, just to hear his voice. I was torn, because it made no sense, but I was so unbelievably happy that he was able to use four words in a sentence, whether they meant anything or not. To this day I have no clue whatsoever what he meant by saying that, but I had to put a meaning behind it, so I made it my e-mail address.

I only smiled when my son smiled, which was not often by any means. Mainly, his expression was one of sadness. When he was a little older, Matthew developed a vocabulary of twenty or so words, and needless to say, the first time he said "Mommy," that was one of the greatest days of my life. I was so overjoyed that he may have recognized me as his mother, and I cried like a baby and wanted to throw the biggest party ever. I had waited four years to hear my son say something most parents hear by the time their child is a year old.

Later that year, I was trying to teach Matthew how to communicate, which was a struggle to say the least. I would look at him and ask, "What is your name?" Of course, he had no response for me. I kept at it for months and months until one day I asked him what his name was once again. Clear as day, in a soft voice he said, "Cricket's the name, Jiminy Cricket." I thought, *Where the hell did that come from?* Then

I realized, *He just used five words in a sentence, even though it was not the answer I was looking for*. My face fell into my hands and once again, I began to cry in pure frustration.

Most of the time my brain was on overload, and my mind hesitated and refused to release any creativity I could use to help my son. After a while, though, it finally did click into my mind: my son was echoing movies that he loved, like *Pinocchio*. I tried to make him understand that his name was Matthew, not Jiminy Cricket, but unfortunately, he couldn't grasp it. Matthew was very repetitive when he spoke, echoing a lot of what other people was saying. That was so very hard for us. Even though it seemed like it took forever, we finally got there, and what a joy that was. This is when all my very hard, difficult, constant work came to fruition. He finally recognized his name.

I then tried to teach him his age. I would ask him how old he was, but he wouldn't respond as usual. So I would tell him that he was four years old. Every question I asked my son, I had to answer for him, as he was not interested in answering for himself. Yet, another difficult obstacle to overcome and to teach him. I kept asking him how old he was for so long, and one day, without focusing on me, he said, "You're four." I thought to myself, *Here we go again*. He was getting his nouns and pronouns confused. For instance, once his vocabulary expanded, he would say, "He wants to go outside and play" instead of "I want to go outside and play." I was so angry and frustrated.

I took a deep breath and asked my son again, "How old are you?" and I got the same answer. As I sat there for a moment and tried to collect my thoughts, I prayed to God to enlighten my mind and my son's mind. Then I tried using a bit of reverse psychology. I asked Matthew the question again and received the same response. I then told him "No, I'm four." After many months of doing this, I again asked him how old he was, and he responded, "I'm four." Finally, a little progress!

We moved on by using flashcards with numbers and letters and colored pictures. He showed such infatuation with numbers, letters, and trains. Matthew did not like many songs, and I could never sing him to sleep because my singing voice annoyed him. It was very heart-wrenching, because I wanted to be near my son. But he would always push me away if I started singing a song he didn't like. I finally figured out that the only way he would allow me to hold him and sing a song was if I made the song about Matthew. I would have to change the words of the song so that it said his name and things about him.

For example, instead of singing, "You are my sunshine," I would sing, "You are my Matthew." He did love watching most Disney movies and also enjoyed listening to Barney songs. These were his favorites, along with the Kid songs videos. He learned quite a bit watching those videos. Each time a new one came out, I went out to buy it. He would remain focused on these videos especially. He would mimic what the young children would say and do. Eventually, though, he outgrew these videos.

One song that really captured Matthew's attention was Whitney Houston's "I Will Always Love You." When it came on the VH1 video channel, he would immediately stop and drop anything he was doing at the time to run to the television to watch and listen to her sing. He would stand so attentively, mesmerized by her. I would think to myself that this was the perfect opportunity for me to hold my son, because he was so focused on her and the song, but as usual he pushed me away. It just broke my heart. As I listened to the song along with him, those tears always came back. When the song was over, he would go right back to whatever he was doing before.

He also really liked the Celine Dion song "Because You Loved Me." That song really relates to my relationship with Matthew, because I was always his voice when he couldn't speak and his eyes when he couldn't see, for so many years. Now whenever I hear those songs, I cry so heartily, because it makes me think of him and how I love him so dearly. They also remind me of what an extreme struggle it was to get through all those hard younger years.

Matthew did like it at times when we read stories to him. He particularly liked the ones with colorful pictures, numbers, and letters, which were visually stimulating and helped him to stay focused. He was a visual learner—although he did also love it when his father talked to him with a Donald Duck voice.

Another challenge we had was when were still trying to potty train Matthew. This had to be our single hardest challenge at this time. Matthew showed no interest in training, and nothing seemed to work until my husband had the idea to put a little piece of colorful construction paper in the toilet and told Matthew to hit it with his urine stream. Matt made a game of it. We then found toilet targets that made potty training a bit easier. However, it still took way too much time. Eventually, though, Matthew got there.

Even something as simple as tying his shoes was very difficult for Matthew. Yet there were some things he could do surprisingly well. My son loved stacking small wooden blocks as high as he could, and it was amazing to see how high he could go and how it had stayed so still while he placed the blocks one by one on top of each other. What great concentration and steady hands my son has.

Another thing that made Matthew happy at this time was getting into our linen closet. He would pull out all the top sheets, towels, and blankets out on to the floor and try to play his game of hide and seek with us. He would sit there quietly on one of the shelves so contentedly, and my husband and I would be there just watching him have a joyous time. We knew he had no concept of how to play normal hide and seek.

Matthew's way of playing hide and seek

At this point, Matthew had to be transferred from his crib to the "big boy bed." We would constantly check in on him during the night. There were two nights where he scared us to death. The first time was when I checked on him during the night as usual, and he was not in his bed. I was frantically looking everywhere for him. I screamed to my husband that I could not find Matthew. He leaped out of bed and I was crying to him and saying, "I can't find Matthew, I can't find our son." I was screaming for him, "Where are you, my Matthew, where are you?"

We looked everywhere, and finally we found that little stinker underneath a table in his room covered up in blankets. When we removed the blankets, there he was, awake and smiling. I was so relieved to have found him, but for God's sake, why did he not respond to us? Why did he put us through such torture? I hugged him and tried to explain that he needed to stay in the big-boy bed and not get off of it in the middle of the night and move to another area—and also, to always answer us immediately when we called out his name.

The second scary situation he put us through came when Matt was checking on him during the night and again he was nowhere to be found. Matt did not respond as frantically as I had. He saw a lot of blankets piled up on Matthew's bed and started to peel them back because he was sure our son was there. But Matthew wasn't. That's when Matt started to panic and yelled for me, saying, "Matthew is nowhere to be found!" We both lost it. I was again looking frantically around Matthew's room screaming out his name.

Matt looked all around the house, and as he also ran to the basement, as we needed to keep the door ajar for the cats we had at that time—their litter box was kept downstairs. Still my Matthew was nowhere to be found. I kept praying and praying to find him. Then we both dropped to our knees. I was praying and crying. Matt looked underneath Matthew's bed, and there, in the far corner under his favorite blanket, was our little boy sleeping away. We must have aged ten years that night with all that stress.

We slowly pulled on his chubby little legs and got him out from underneath the bed and placed him on top of the bed. To our surprise, he slept through this whole process. At this point, we had no choice but for one of us to sleep on his bedroom floor until we felt safe enough for him to sleep in his bed on his own.

I have to say, if ever there was the perfect man to have Matthew with and to be the father of my child, it would be my husband. Matt has always been in our son's life and has never given up or abandoned us. I have seen so many families torn apart and been at support groups where one parent has given up. The percentage rate of married couples with autistic children divorcing is said to be extremely high, which is unfortunate because the children need the support of both parents. My husband and I have always fought for our son, and we will continue to fight for him for the rest of our lives. Today, we have been married for twenty-two and a half years.

I met my husband when I was twenty-one and he was twenty. After dating a while, I realized how much he liked to drink alcohol. This caused problems in our relationship, and I knew I wasn't going to marry someone with a drinking problem. After one night of heavy drinking, he was driving home alone and fell asleep at the wheel, and he hit a parked truck. Thank God no one was injured.

Matt woke up immediately and thought he had collided with a trash can, but it was really a parked truck on the other side of the street. This was a wakeup call for him. The next morning, he called me and told me he needed to see me. At this time, we weren't dating as often because of his drinking. When I saw the truck, I immediately hugged him and asked if anyone had been injured. He said no, but told me that he needed help to stop drinking. We then went to a hospital to get him detoxified and to get him the help he was so desperately seeking, although he was afraid to admit it to himself.

I am happy to say as of October 27, 2013, my husband will have been sober for twenty-six years. Matt and I dated off and on for nine years before we got married. I waited four years to marry him because I wanted to be certain he would not relapse. I am so proud of him. He had more willpower than I could ever imagine. I was so scared that when Matthew was diagnosed with autism, my husband would relapse, but by the grace of God he didn't. I cannot express how amazed I am by his willpower. I am so proud of him for accomplishing such a hard thing through an even harder situation.

It would bring us to tears when Matt could not play ball with his son. Matt would also want to take Matthew fishing, but all Matthew would want to do was throw rocks in the water. There was only a couple of ways we could get his attention—blowing bubbles for hours and sitting where the trains went by.

My husband would go for daily walks with Matthew. On one particular walk they went a little bit farther down this certain street about a mile away from the house where the railroad tracks ran parallel. We would usually stop so we could see the trains go by. As my husband describes it:

On this walk and during the wait for the train to end, I got to thinking, *Why is my son so fascinated by trains? Was it the engines or the noise of the passing boxcars? Or is he simply waiting for the line of cars to go by?* We would often see many of the same people on our walks. This time, we had made a special stop at a friend of mine's house. Their house just happened to be by the railroad tracks and a busy intersection. We would sit for hours on end on a specific stone patiently watching the cars go by and seeing the people wave to Matthew. My friend would bring two bottles of water and one small candy bar out to Matthew. He loved this.

When it was time to go, it was very difficult. We went through a ritual that I called the countdown. I would say, 'Matthew, we have five minutes before we have to start walking.' Then I would count down the minutes: five, four, three, two, one, and then it became the time to leave. This made the walks so much easier, because there was no fighting, no redirecting, no temper tantrums, and no meltdowns. We were finally starting to connect.

I remember one year in our neighborhood, there was a major construction project going on. He would love to walk by and see all the dump trucks and cranes. All this movement, noise, and dust fascinated my son. Over the months of summer, we spent many days watching the guys at work. Many of them knew us and would come over to say hi to my little guy. A father never felt more proud to see his son recognized.

These walks gave me time to think about life and what it would hold for my son. How would he do in school? Would he have lots of friends? Would our house be the house for sleepovers? What about his grades? Would teachers like him? Will he be a good student? All these were such overwhelming thoughts to a young father. And all this, was before we knew our special son had autism.

Chapter 2

Autism Diagnosis

Family members and friends kept assuring us that boys just take longer to develop, and we should give Matthew more time. He still showed absolutely no eye contact and would only stay focused on something that interested him—something he did on his own terms. When I could get Matthew to look at me (which was not very often), I knew he was only looking through me and not focusing on me. He was completely absorbed in his own little world. I was just irritating him. This was so heartbreaking.

Finally, I called my son's pediatrician. The doctor told me he wanted to see Matthew right away. I was so frightened to go to this appointment. I knew in my heart there was something seriously wrong. But what could it possibly be? My mother went with me because I would need a lot of support and Matt was working. Taking Matthew anywhere was a challenge, and we were having a difficult time in the doctor's office. I was trying so hard to calm him down and listen to what the doctor had to say.

Matthew's doctor mentioned the possibility of autism. My mother heard the doctor say this, and it was devastating to her—she knew her daughter and son-in-law had a rough road ahead of them. But since I was having such a difficult time trying to calm my son down, it went right over my head. My whole mind was concentrating on my son. The doctor advised us to have Matthew evaluated, which we did immediately.

On May 23, 1995, at 3:30 in the afternoon, after a full day of testing, we got the devastating diagnosis of autism for Matthew. That horrible day will forever be embedded in our minds. At this time, the doctors told us that autism was associated with mental retardation and that our son might not amount to much in life. We were then given a list of institutions they suggested we put him in. Needless to say, my husband and I were devastated. I ran over to my son and tried to hug him, tears flowing, but as usual he pulled away from me.

We told the doctors that Matthew was going nowhere but home with us, but to please explain what autism was and how we would go about starting to help our very special son. Autism, we learned, is a brain-development disorder that impairs social interaction and communication, causing restricted and repetitive behavior. There is no cure. Needless to say, the ride home was the worst we ever took. My husband was driving, and I was in the back seat with Matthew. Matt and I were both crying. We were so lost and sad, wondering what was in store for our lives and the future of our son. I tried to focus on how to generate hope and have the wisdom. How was I going to get through all of the despair, depression, negative moods, and sadness? My mental events of dealing with autism everyday would just draw me down deeper into depression. How do I get through all of this? I needed to maintain a positive outlook; trying very hard to stay upbeat, this task was extremely difficult, most of the time. With lots of prayers and support, I was able to cope. Although, I found that I was judging and evaluating myself and would wonder why I was not measuring up to be the mother, I needed to be. How was I going to find a way with all of the autism chain of events that led me to persistent unhappiness? I tried everything to avoid issues that would lead me down that path.

I needed to remain focused on my challenges I was facing, at that moment and all the challenges that were ahead of me. All of the hardships I was dealing with everyday required that I learn how to conquer them sufficiently. I needed to learn and remain focused without fear and anxiety, just because my son would not comprehend the task that I was trying to teach him on that day, quickly enough. What I noticed and found important, is to select one thing at a time and focus all of my attention to just that particular objective. I found myself becoming impatient at times because I had so much I needed to teach him about our world. Many things just took up too much valuable time.

I also found I was judging myself harshly because I was not making as much progress with my son as I thought I should be making. I felt I needed to complete my goals for my son quickly and effectively. However, dealing with autism, nothing comes quickly. My expectations for my son did not come soon enough, and I was constantly disappointed and irritated with my efforts, not knowing the exact teaching methods for my son. I desperately needed to make progress. I was so lost and confused, which made the situation more difficult for my emotions, which I was feeling and dealing with on an everyday basis.

I could not allow my mind to wander but instead to just remain focused otherwise I would become negative and self-critical to myself, which would interfere and pull me down. With every difficult obstacle we came across and conquered with my son, he persevered. Oh, how I praised him, each and every time.

Eventually, I realized I knew I should not be so judgmental about myself, and just realize, I was doing the best I could and no matter how long it took to teach him, as long as he learned it. I always prayed everyday to have some sort of success with my son. No matter if it was a large or small accomplishment.

My husband and I both are from very large families. My parents have eleven children, and my husband's parents have ten children. There was no autism on either side of our families. We even went back as far as our family trees and did genetic research to see if anyone had autism in either of our families. Nothing was found. We thought maybe autism was hereditary. Is it? We didn't know. All we knew was our son had autism. Where did it come from? Why did it happen? Was it something I did while I was pregnant? So many unanswered questions. I felt someone or something should be held accountable for our distress. Or maybe it was merely God's will. If it was indeed God's will, we would be more accepting of that.

When Matthew was born, I was so happy and looking forward to being a new mother. When we brought our baby home, all he did was cry constantly like he was in great pain. My motherly instinct told me something wasn't right, but I convinced myself that most newborns do cry a lot and it would eventually come to an end. As he got a little older, the crying not only continued but grew worse. Now he began to scream—not just a scream, but a *bloodcurdling* screaming, full of agony. At this time, Matthew had most of his required vaccinations given to him at his pediatrician's office. With all the controversy surrounding vaccinations today, I wish I knew if they were a contributing factor to my son's autism. I hope and pray that in my lifetime, I find the answer as to why my son is autistic. I never wanted my son on any type of medication. I told myself I can do this without medicating my child. I did not want him to be like a zombie or just in a daze, which I thought in my opinion, medication would do to him. Some family members would see a lot of my frustration I was having and told me to maybe address this issue with his pediatrician and maybe something might help to alleviate some of the distress and most importantly, possibly help my Matthew.

At this point, I was so desperate that I went ahead and spoke with my son's doctor, and we did try a few medications. I thought it is only natural that medication might be vital. However, nothing seemed to work well for my son. I felt if it wasn't helping, I was not going to give it to him. I again spoke with my son's doctor and we eliminated the medication. The doctor recommended trying something different. I did not want to do it, however I did tell the doctor if I changed my mind, I would let the doctor know. I began researching for other alternatives. I found that some vitamins helped him function better. My son has never been on any medications since then, except for an antibiotic for any ailment he had.

Matthew was infatuated with trains; something we learned was not unusual for kids with autism. My husband's parents lived right next door to my parents (that's how Matt and I first met). The homes were near a railroad crossing, and there was a train track less than a block from their houses. Matthew loved sitting on their porches as the trains went by. He loved the numbers on the trains and the noise they made. Some people with autism do not like the distraction of loud noises, but this was not a problem for Matthew. The longer the trains were, the more he liked them. As he watched, his head would stay focused, but his eyes would move rapidly with the boxcars.

The start of Matthew's interest in trains

Routine was also important to Matthew. Every day at the same time, he and I would take ten trips around our block. Each time we passed our house, we would count. On one particular day, we were on our seventh trip around the block when a bird decided to leave its droppings in my hair, right on top of my head. I bent down, looked at Matthew, pointed to what had happened, and told him we needed to go home and that Mom needed to get in the shower right away to get the bird waste out of her hair. He did not care, nor did he understand what I was saying; he was so focused and intent on his routine walk. We started to walk toward the house, and Matthew began to scream and cry. I had to pick him up with all the strength I had—he was kicking and hitting me, trying to escape from my grasp. We finally made it into the house. After my shower, we started our ten trips around the block all over again.

Most of those days also involved sitting on a big rock by the train tracks watching the trains go by for several hours at a time. Again, I found myself so depressed. I would sit there crying and crying, wondering why he couldn't be a typical child.

Whenever we were going somewhere, I had to give Matthew time intervals. For example, I would say, "Matthew, in ten minutes, we are going to be leaving." Then I would say, "Matthew, in five minutes, we are going to be leaving," and so on. This made the transition to leaving a bit easier.

There was one particular time we were going to the grocery store, and the route we usually took was closed for construction. I had to take a detour. Matthew instantly started screaming and crying. I had absolutely no idea what had caused this meltdown to happen all of a sudden, just out of nowhere. I pulled over the car and crawled into the backseat, but I saw nothing wrong. I kept asking my son what was wrong, but of course he was unable to communicate with me. I tried hugging him to comfort him, but again he only pulled away. How many more times would my heart have to break? After being in the backseat for a little while, I managed somehow to get him calm. Later on, it finally clicked in my mind that Matthew was screaming and crying because taking a different route was out of routine, and that really upset him.

I was starting to feel like a robot instead of a mother, because all Matthew had to do was make a peep and my buttons would be pushed. Most autistics need a specific routine to function well. However, I really wanted to change that with Matthew. As things in life happen and can happen in an instant, we had to teach him how to adapt to these quick changes.

When we finally got to the grocery store that day it was very busy, so I had to park farther away from the entrance than I normally would have. Matthew had to stop at each and every car and read every one of the license-plate numbers and letters. It took us forever to get to the store entrance, but I didn't care because I got to hear my son's voice as he read all of the numbers and letters.

While shopping in a store, Matthew loved to pick up an item and look for the letters in the ingredients and say the letters. The bigger the words, the more fascinated Matthew became because of all the letters in the word. Needless to say, grocery shopping took forever to complete.

When we were almost done, we passed the helium balloons, which Matthew just loved. I would occasionally buy one for Matthew, not only to make him happy but to make the transition of leaving the store much more pleasant. On this day, Matthew reached for one of the balloons and I told him that he couldn't have one this time. He started screaming and crying, and I calmly tried to comfort him. Two women passed us in an aisle and said that if Matthew was their son, he would not be acting that way. My heart just sank. They had no idea of my struggles and hardships. I was very pissed at them for saying that to me and allowing me to hear it.

I looked at Matthew and said, "We are not going to let those bitches get away with that." In that instant, Matthew stopped crying and was completely calm—like he had a sense of how angry I was. As we went down the next aisle, I saw the two women. I walked up to them and told them it was none of their business, but my son had autism, and the next time they decided they wanted to open up their mouths and say something so rude because they are so ignorant and quick to judge, they should know that they are the type of people who make it so very hard for parents of children with disabilities. I continued to say that the next time they decided to open up their filthy mouths; I highly suggested they remember their experience with me. I left them by saying, "I did not ask for my child to be autistic."

The whole time I was talking, they stood silent, in total shock. I hope they learned their lesson and would never, ever do that to anyone else. That's how it went most of the time wherever we went. People would either roll their eyes, make rude remarks, or do something to let us know they were disgusted with us. I was constantly sticking up for my child, never speaking meanly to the rude ones—not that I didn't want to, and not that they didn't deserve it. I would speak to them calmly, maintaining self-control, but with a firm attitude and a stern tone.

Most of the time when we were out and Matthew had yet another meltdown episode; we would just get up and leave. Finally, one day, I decided that I'd had enough, and we were not going to leave. We did everything in our power to help Matthew remain calm, so we were not too badly disruptive to others.

However, there were nice people out there. Every week we would take Matthew to a local hot-dog shop and sit in a booth by the window so he could watch the trains go by while he ate. One day when we went there, Matthew ran to that same booth, but it was occupied by a couple. Chaos broke out as Matthew started screaming because someone was already sitting where we normally sat. The couple in the booth asked us if there was a problem, so once again I had to explain that Matthew was autistic and that we usually sat at that booth. I then apologized for the interruption and said that we were just going to leave. That very kind couple told us we did not have to leave and they would gladly move to another booth so we could accommodate Matthew. That really touched our hearts deeply. It made me realize that there are still good people out there. I couldn't believe that right in the middle of their dinner, they were willing to pick up everything and go to another booth just to accommodate my son.

Another thing I remember about eating out with Matthew is how much he loved McDonald's. He would always get a Happy Meal plain hamburger. The thing I remember most, though, is that when I would try to hand Matthew the Happy Meal bag, he would start screaming furiously. I could not fathom why he was reacting with such great fear. Finally, I realized he was afraid of the bag, the hamburger wrapper, and the pouch the French fries came in. I don't know if it was because he hated the noise they made, but this went on for years. I would always have to put the food on a plate so he could eat it.

Eventually, I told him he had to take the food out of the bag himself, and after arguing with me for quite some time, he finally did it. I had to get him to overcome this fear. Why would something as simple as a hamburger wrapper or fry pouch terrorize my son so badly? I had to put a stop to this. It may have been one of his many sensory issues. Another issue was Matthew would only eat with a fork, even if it was soup. Also, the silverware had to have no design on it or he would scream in frustration and wanted a plain looking utensil. Needless to say all my silverware had some type of design on it and I had to go out and buy more utensils that Matthew felt comfortable with using. Still today he prefers to use just a fork with anything he eats but now, it can have any design on it.

When Matthew was younger, around Christmastime, things would get very hard. I tried to ask Matthew what he wanted for Christmas, but he would never respond because he had little to no vocabulary. Did he even understand what we were asking him? Some parents would tell me how lucky I was that my child wasn't asking for hundreds of gifts like their children were, and this would get me so angry because they were the lucky ones. They had a child who could communicate and tell them what he or she wanted. I didn't care how expensive or absurd it was. I just wanted to be able to hear my son speak and tell me what he wanted for Christmas. Now he has a true concept of what Christmas is all about and that the most important part of this special day is that it's the day Jesus was born. It's not just about receiving presents.

Going back to buying gifts for him, I had to play a guessing game, and I usually picked out things that had numbers and letters on them since we knew Matthew like these types of toys, and they would capture Matthew's attention. He also loved memorizing facts, but only on his terms. What interested him the most were the rubber numbers-and-letters floor sets. I would give Matthew a number or letter and tell him to place it where it belonged. He would always get it right. This made us very happy because it felt normal.

I used his love of numbers and letters to my advantage. I told him I would count to ten if he hugged me while I counted. He allowed this to happen, to my surprise. I treasured every moment of those hugs. I tried to mix up the numbers, just to see if he was paying close attention to me. For example: When I was counting the numbers and was reaching to the last highest number, I would start again by saying one, two, and three. No way was Matthew going to let me get away with that. He caught on to that right away and would say no and then tell me the exact number where we left off. I just wanted more attention from my precious son; I wanted more than ten seconds of his loving hugs. Matthew started to read sooner than most children, probably because of his extreme love for letters.

There was another frightening incident, which my husband kept from me because he knew how angry I would be about it. When Matthew was around seven years old, he and his father needed to go to the lumberyard and pick up some wood trim for a door that Matt was fixing. Matthew was old enough now to ride in the front seat of the car. The trim had to be laid down in the car, so this of course involved folding the backseat down. Matthew was unaware that this could be done. However, he was very observant watching his father folding down the backseat, where Matthew usually rode in the car.

They completed their project and decided a little later to take a quick trip to the store. My husband parked the car in front of the store and ran in quickly by himself, locking Matthew in the car. By the time my husband returned to the car moments later, there was no Matthew to be found. My husband was totally hysterical. He knew he had locked Matthew in the car and there was no way for our boy to get out. So he unlocked the car door screaming for Matthew in the front and backseats, and then all of a sudden the backseat came folding down and out pops my son's head saying, "Dad, I was in the trunk."

Matt, gasping for air, with tears in his eyes, told our son, "Don't ever, ever do that to your father again, and don't ever tell your mother about this, ever." That was some wrong advice to give to Matthew. I eventually did find out because most people with autism are very honest and my son did end up telling me. And my husband really regrets not telling me about this frightening experience sooner. However, I was so glad that everything had turned out all right.

Around the third grade, Matthew started participating in spelling contests at his school. Also by this time, he had memorized all of the US presidents, the years they served in office, their wives' names, and which ones were assassinated during their term. He also memorized all of the states and capitals and the years they joined the Union. Eventually, no matter where we went, Matthew would insist on having a dictionary or telephone book in his hand. This continued through his early teenage years. At that point, it was yet another struggle to communicate to him that taking the telephone book or dictionary may seem inappropriate or odd to people. After getting Matthew to recognize this, he started just carrying around small pictures, whether it would be of family members, trains or his spell bowl pictures. This lasted a few more years. Today, he no longer carries anything like that with him; he carries only his wallet and keys.

As autism took over my entire life, I would ask myself, *Oh my God, what else am I in for? When will we be able to live a normal life? Is that ever going to be possible for us?* By the time Matthew was a little older, I became stronger and wiser. I had been his voice for so long. I began to really learn about autism, and as a parent of a child with a disability, I also learned to appropriately fight for what was best for my son. Parents who live with autism 24/7 are the experts, as they live with it on a daily basis.

Matthew at that time had a tendency to bite things or people and to push other children. This was so frightening, and I had to keep such a close watch on him at all times. Which I always did anyways, but the tragedy that could have had happened scared me the most. For us as his parents, had he hurt anyone, this would have been so traumatic and devastating. (Thank God he never did. I must have been doing a good job to ensure that this never happened.) I always praised my son when he conquered anything that was appropriate. This always made Matthew happy, which in return made us happy.

One of the bright spots for Matthew was that he enjoyed therapeutic horseback riding. Once a week during the summer months, we would take him to a place in the country that offered horseback riding for children and adults with disabilities. How Matthew enjoyed this! One time the trainers put him on a horse and slowly stood him up on the saddle. Looking on in pure amazement, we could not believe how he stood so still with his arms out from his sides. I was so scared he would fall, but he had such a look of confidence and balance and happiness at what he had accomplished. The huge smile on his face said, *Look at me, Mom and Dad, and see what I can do!* My son showed no fear. He truly loved those horses.

Matthew's therapeutic horseback riding

There was one other thing that really captured Matthew's attention at this time—when his father would watch NASCAR racing. How Matthew enjoyed watching those fast cars go by! His reaction would be to hand-flap so furiously that at times we thought he would break his wrist bones. The house would literally vibrate from the exciting emotions of the hand-flapping. Items atop the television would be moved by the momentum of the hand-flapping, not to mention the facial expression that came along with the utter excitement. So, since 2009, Matthew and his father have been going to the NASCAR race at the brickyard every year, and what a joy it is to see my husband and son have a most wonderful time enjoying a father-and-son day together.

Chapter 3

School and Learning

After the autism diagnosis, the experts suggested we put Matthew into a developmental preschool right away. We made an appointment for Matthew to be seen by a disabilities director to find a placement. My husband, my lovely mother, and I all went to the meeting. As my husband and I were talking to the director, my mother noticed that Matthew would walk back and forth along a row of windows. A psychologist in the office told my mother that was a sure sign of autism. I immediately got a hold of the preschool and enrolled my son right away.

The administrators suggested I take Matthew to extra speech therapy. So I took him to a speech therapist at our local hospital. This was an extremely difficult process. I took Matthew there three days a week for an hour-long session. We sat in a tiny room while the therapist tried to work with Matthew, but all he would do was scream and cry. He was very uncooperative. By the time we left, I would be drenched in sweat from trying to get him to cooperate.

Matthew was three when he started at the developmental preschool. I was extremely nervous about this. It was hard for me to trust anyone but my family and my husband's family with my son. Every day, I would drop Matthew off at the school and pick him up afterward.

One day when I walked into the school to pick him up, I heard him screaming. I ran to the classroom door and looked in. To my surprise and dismay, I saw one of the assistants yelling at my son as he shivered in fear in a corner. I froze in shock as I watched her grab him by the arms and jerk him up from the floor. This happened so quickly. I ran into that room and put my son behind myself. Then I looked that woman square in the eyes—nose to nose—and told her she would never, ever touch my son again and that I would do whatever it took to make sure she never worked at any school ever again.

I immediately reported her to the school system. I'm not sure what ever came of that, but I hope she was fired. Because autism had taken over my entire life, I never got the chance to follow through and make sure that was done. I needed to put all my effort toward my son rather than toward a stupid person who, in my opinion, had no business working with special-needs children. I feel very guilty, because how many more special-needs children did that person hurt? I hope she learned her lesson and never did it again.

By the time this happened, there were only a few more weeks of preschool to complete. The head teacher of the classroom, who I felt a little more at ease with, promised me she would keep an extra-close eye on my son and would not let that worker who abused my son near him, and that she would be the only one to work with my son. I was torn as to what to do.

I let him finish out the school year. I often wonder if I made a horrible mistake there. I truly believe, when looking back on that time, that there was more abuse than I was aware of. Another day the speech therapist called and told me that Matthew had fallen out of the therapeutic swing that sat in the classroom. This seemed almost impossible to me, because the children were secured by a bar when in the swing. My motherly instincts told me that he did not fall out of the swing, but that they struck him, abused him with something, and that is what gave him this huge bumpy bruise on his forehead.

After that nightmare was over, I located a new developmental preschool that offered him a five-day-a-week program. This was a little bit easier, because they provided a program assistant and I got to meet and speak with her. It was very important to me to know exactly who would be working with my son. I felt she had a genuine caring for my son and his well-being. She also was willing to stay in touch with me through a communication book. We talked on a regular basis. Also, she allowed me to call her as frequently as I needed to talk about my son's progress.

This program assistant told me that at times Matthew would be disruptive during class, and the teacher would prefer to just send Matthew out into the hallway to sit there instead of allowing my son to take a short learning break, even if it was just walking around the school and trying to interact with his program assistant. As far as I was told, the program assistant said that did not happen a lot. To me, once was too many times. I spoke with the teacher and told her that this was unacceptable and would not be tolerated and that I would be keeping a close eye on what was going on at the preschool.

Things seemed to get a little better after that, especially when I would just show up, which I did unexpectedly and took them off guard. I did this to protect my son and keep the teachers aware that at any time, I could be there. I was allowed to do this at this particular preschool.

I do have to give credit to this program assistant, as I think she did the best she could and was mostly honest with me. I am pretty sure of that. However, we were so glad when those developmental nightmare schooldays were over for our son. Matthew was so excited to start kindergarten and to ride the bus to school. He was mainstreamed into a normal classroom setting with a very good program assistant to help him throughout his half day of kindergarten. She would take

Matthew from the classroom if he needed a break or was disruptive to the other children, who were also there trying to learn.

I did express my opinion in the beginning that Matthew should stay in the classroom as much as possible and to only remove him if he was being loud or disruptive for any reason. I felt comfortable with his kindergarten program assistant. The year seemed to go a little more smoothly, and I felt more at ease that no abuse was taking place. At least, I hoped not.

After kindergarten, we moved out of that school district and entered a new one. I was apprehensive about being in a new district, but we were fortunate to have a program director that was very good. Meeting her at the IEP (Individualized Education Plan) conference put me much more at ease. She knew and understood my concerns and accommodated them as best she could.

Starting with the first grade, Matthew had a program assistant who was the greatest of all. She was with him all the way through fifth grade. She was an exceptional program assistant and really cared for my son and his well-being. When my son went off to middle school, we had to say good-bye to her. This was so very difficult. Could I ever trust another program assistant like I did her? Why did we even have to go through that? We still maintain a relationship with her to this day. She always remembers Matthew's birthday and is so loving and caring to my special son.

Matthew's program assistant was truly amazing. She allowed me to call her at home. Whenever Matthew was disruptive, she would gently take him outside and walk him around the school, while talking with him and teaching him. Every time there was a sewer grate, they would stop so Matthew could throw a rock into it. This routine made transitioning back into the classroom so much easier for him.

All through elementary school, Matthew had a sensory issue with clothing. He would only wear sweatpants and sweatshirts that had numbers or letters on them. He would not wear button-down shirts. We thanked God that he would keep his clothes on at school, because a lot of autistics don't. But the moment we got home, he would strip down to his boxers.

When Matthew was about seven years old, we signed him up for Little League. Every child had a chance to play each position, but Matthew always wanted to bat. He didn't understand the concept of sharing, and he would get very angry when he wasn't allowed to do that. It would get to the point where we had to remove him from the field. He didn't seem to enjoy it, so we finished out that year and didn't sign him up again.

The transition from elementary school to middle school was not as difficult as we feared. We had all summer to prepare, and we were experienced by now and knew how to use our time constructively. The sensory issue was still there, but Matthew would agree to wear plain shirts. He still did not like button-down shirts and would only wear sweatpants. In middle school, we were fortunate to once again have program assistants who worked well with Matthew.

Around this time, Matthew needed glasses, and we were afraid of how he would react to having to wear them on a constant basis. He adapted very well, to our surprise. He looked so adorable with his new glasses. We would call him our little Harry Potter, as he so resembled the character at that time.

A few years later, when Matthew needed braces, I again worried about what his reaction would be and if he could tolerate this change and the pain. Wearing braces myself when I was older because of TMJ, I knew how much those braces hurt at first until you got used to them. As with the glasses, Matthew adapted surprisingly well. He did complain of the pain for a short while. At one point, he even told me he wanted them off his teeth. I explained that the pain would not last forever and would eventually go away. His teeth just needed a chance to adjust. He always did have a high tolerance for certain types of pain, though. While playing, he would fall down sometimes and get right back up, say "I am okay," and continue to play.

We would always ask Matthew questions and see what his answers were. Sometimes, he answered correctly; other times, he did not. So, back to explaining it again, over and over, until it was totally absorbed in his mind and he knew exactly what we were saying and what we were trying to teach him.

During his early school years, trying to have a conversation with Matthew was extremely difficult—as was homework and many other things. He would always complain and say, "It's going to be a long talk." I would try to explain to him that it would not be such a long conversation if he would just sit and listen without complaining, but he didn't comprehend that. He preferred to argue about the situation. It did not matter what we were talking about—whether we were trying to teach him right from wrong, explain certain areas of how life works, or have a conversation about school. He just preferred to argue with us. Not only were we raising an autistic child, but when he was becoming a teenager, we were also dealing with an autistic young man with a typical teenage attitude.

We just wanted to communicate with our son, but the only way for us to accomplish that was to sit outside of his room and listen to him converse with himself before he went to bed at night. This is how we found out most of our information about our son. And this was the only way we got most of our answers to the questions we tried to ask him. My son would talk to himself and then sometimes also answer himself. This could go on for hours, and there we were, camped outside his bedroom door, listening very intently.

I noticed that whenever I took a picture of Matthew, he looked so sad, or he was crying in the picture and had dark circles under his eyes. Also, his skin was so pale. Looking back, I believe that this was because Matthew was so full of metal toxins.

Matthew was such a loner. I always wondered, *Will we ever be able to sit down like a family and have a simple dinner with conversation? Will we ever be able to just have family night and play a board game?* This did not happen until he was much older. Sometimes he still prefers doing his own thing.

Whenever my husband and I would get hurt physically (nothing major, thank God), Matthew would never, ever recognize this or appear to care. He just walked away, laughed, or ignored us. This also brought much concern. What if, God forbid, something serious did happen to us? What would our son do?

This was a very important issue, and the time came to teach him all about serious things that can happen in a split second. He had to know what to do. We taught him about calling for help if Mom or Dad, or anyone he was with, could not get up and was unconscious. It was a very difficult obstacle to teach him this; we had to talk to him constantly about it and remind him what to do. Today, he has full understanding and is constantly watching out for us and others. For example, if I am taking a shower and he hears me drop the bar of soap, Matthew will knock on the door and yell, "Mom, are you all right?" More great progress! Today my son shows his parents and family members much love and concern. He is always willing to hug and give a hello or goodbye cheek kiss. He will even ask me how my day went, how I am feeling, and will address me in saying good morning or goodnight. I never thought that would ever happen. I was elated in having such great communication with my dear son. Significant progress!

When Matthew was a preteen, his Grandma DeGeyter passed away. At the viewing, I was in the front row with Grandpa DeGeyter and Matthew as we sat praying for Grandma DeGeyter and looking at her at peace. Matthew was seated between us. All of a sudden, Matthew looked at Grandpa DeGeyter and said, "Grandpa, when is Grandma going to wake up?" Grandpa DeGeyter and I both starting crying even more, and I told my father-in-law that I was very sorry my son said that, and he must not quite understand what was actually was happening.

His grandfather just put his arms around Matthew and said, "My special grandson, your grandma is in heaven with God now. She is awake in heaven." Matthew just sat there and nodded to his grandfather, like he understood.

Approximately three years after that very sad event, Grandpa DeGeyter passed away. Matthew even read one of the prayers during the funeral service at church. This time, I believe Matthew had a concept of what had happened. As he told me, "Grandma and Grandpa DeGeyter are now both in heaven with God." I told him he was right and to always pray for them and remember all the wonderful times they spent together.

In yet another tragedy, my father, Grandpa Powell, recently passed away. Matthew has full knowledge of what all this means now. He told me that Grandpa Powell was up in heaven with God too. He said that he prays for his grandpa Powell all the time and remembers all the wonderful times they shared. He tells me that he misses, loves, and prays for my father very much, just like he prays for his other grandparents. I am so very fortunate to still have my lovely mother with me today, and with the grace of God, she will remain with us for many, many years to come.

My husband and I are both from Catholic families, so we wanted to raise our special child in the Catholic faith. At one time we had assumed that Matthew would go to a Catholic school, but parochial schools were not able to accommodate his special needs or provide the services he needed the way the public schools did. So we enrolled Matthew in Catholic education classes for his religious training.

Matthew started the classes when he started kindergarten and continued them until eighth grade. For the first five years, I would have to explain Matthew's situation to the religious-education teacher and stay in the classroom with him. When Matthew was a little older, I was able to sit in the hallway instead of staying in the classroom. However, I still needed to be there in case Matthew was disruptive, as there were typical children there to learn as well and I had no business taking that learning experience away from them, just because of my son's autism. The tears would start to flow every time I would have to do this.

I was so envious of other parents who could simply drop their children off. When I was alone in the hallway and class had begun, I would sit there quietly crying to myself and praying and wondering why things could not just be normal for us as well. Why could I not just simply drop off my child like the other parents were able to do? I was always feeling so alone, scared, sad, and extremely angry. All of these emotions were overwhelming to me.

Regardless of my situation and what it took, my son ended up doing nine years of religious education classes. Matthew made his first reconciliation, first Holy Communion, and his Confirmation. A little time after that, he was even an altar boy at Mass for a few years, and he continues to go to church with us today. We hold on to our faith so tightly.

Matthew started wearing button-down shirts during high school. He still mainly preferred wearing sweatpants, but occasionally he would wear blue jeans because he could put his wallet in the pocket and that made him feel older. Before Matthew entered high school, we started letting him stay home for short periods at a time by himself, keeping in contact with him very regularly. Now we can leave him home all day by himself with little to no worry. At this time Matthew would even start make decisions for himself.

When Matthew started high school, he felt nervous and very apprehensive. There were approximately 2,500 kids enrolled in that high school when Matthew was there, and there were just about 937 students in his senior class alone. The noise of the students in the hallway very much annoyed Matthew, which seemed odd to my husband and I because he loved listening to loud trains. Having such busy hallways made him feel rushed, because he only had seven minutes between classes. He never once used a locker in high school because there was no time to stop between classes. He was so worried about being late to class because he didn't want to be marked tardy.

Matthew would always prepare himself for a full day of school, because he had class all day and then went to Spell Bowl practice or to competitions. At this time, he was becoming much more independent. More great progress on the way, thank God. He loved Spell Bowl so much. When he first started, he felt overwhelmed because he had to know so many words. Each year he was on the team, he had to know over 3,500 words. He was required to write each word twice over the summer to be prepared for the upcoming year of Spell Bowl. Having to know that many words made him feel strained, because it was so many words in so little time, but every time he learned a new word he felt more confident. He felt more and more comfortable with each season.

His teammates became friends, and they would joke around together. As each season went on, they formed a bond that made them work even harder as a team. They won three state championships, in 2006, 2008, and 2009. Helping to win the state championships made Matthew feel extremely proud, because he had accomplished so much. He was even sent a congratulatory letter signed by the state representatives, clerk of the house, and speaker of the house from our state's General Assembly for the 2009 state championship title he helped the team win.

Matthew had a perfect score in Spell Bowl his senior year, meaning he did not misspell one word. Also that year, he was co-captain of the team. Matthew tried his personal best to possess leadership qualities. As co-captain, he had to make sure the team was staying on task, writing words, and being productive. He was on the Spell Bowl team all four years in high school. During his senior year of Spell Bowl, he was also awarded a very prestigious award for team spirit, named after a former Spell Bowl champ. His room is filled with at least a hundred awards proudly displayed from all his accomplishments throughout his entire spelling career, which he started with spelling competitions in third grade.

Matthew also very much enjoyed a theater class he took in high school. In this class, he would do in-class assignments, which were either group-oriented or individual. His favorite assignment was one where he had to act like a mime. This was his favorite because it demonstrated real-life situations. Also during high school, Matthew sometimes had a hard time communicating with people and understanding assignments. When this happened, he would try so hard to clarify things with the person or ask for extra help.

He wanted to have friends but had a hard time with this. He wasn't even sure how to go about making friends. Unfortunately, like many children, he was made fun of. The way I think my son handled this was blocking them out and taking much of his frustration out on us when he got home. Sometimes he just didn't care what they thought of him, as he knew he was doing the best he could.

Doing homework at home was a nightmare at times. He wanted to do the work, but he couldn't put forth the right amount of effort because his mind was distracted by other things. Perhaps the ones who were terrorizing him at school? Even through all of those hardships, we are so very proud to say that Matthew graduated in 2010 with a Core 40 diploma. This diploma means my son took extra courses in general studies that he would need to build his academic foundation to receive success in a four year college or university, or for any apprenticeship program.

High school graduation picture 2010

Matthew took driver's education classes and now has his driver's license. My son also has a job, where he has been at for almost three years now. I have always told Matthew to do his personal best and that giving up was never, ever an option. You must work very, very hard to achieve your goals.

Matthew is now enrolled in a community college where he is taking general-education classes. We are hoping to transfer those credits to a four-year college where he can start his major, whatever that may be. He still keeps changing his mind. He has very high goals, as we also do for him.

One lesson Matthew did have to learn the hard way is that not everyone can be trusted. A fellow college student approached him as he was waiting to go to his next class and asked to borrow one of his very expensive textbooks. This young man told Matthew he needed the book to study for an upcoming test and did not have his copy readily available. My son was torn as to what to do. Part of him knew not to lend the book, but the other part told him it would be okay, because I've always taught him to treat others as he wants to be treated. So he loaned the man the book and made a plan to pick it up the next day in the library. The next day Matthew arrived at the library, but the young man never showed up.

Thankfully, after numerous phones calls and reaching out to someone, we were able to find Matthew a new book. He will never do that again. I explained to Matthew that there are good people in the world and, unfortunately, bad people in the world. He must learn how to differentiate between the two. That is by no means an easy thing to learn.

At this time, since Matthew was communicating better, we decided to write a list of questions and see how he would answer them. Here are some of those questions we asked him along with his responses:

1. What are your strengths? "I try to work well under pressure and doing my personal best at work and at college."

2. What are your weaknesses? "Trying to stay on task and meeting deadlines. Trying to be better at maintaining self-control."

3. What kind of people do you like? "I like nice respectful people like myself. People who are thoughtful and always thinking about others, before themselves."

4. How would you describe your personality? "I would consider myself thoughtful, courteous, polite and caring."

5. What kind of people do you dislike? "I dislike people who disrespect me, that are liars, cheaters, very

selfish, conceited people and the most of all; I dislike people who are manipulators."

6. Are you ambitious? "I would consider myself very ambitious because I want to get the most out of life. Nothing comes free. I am always trying to better myself in college and on my job."

7. What makes you angry? "Being lied to, making a simple mistake that I shouldn't have made, I must always remember to think before I speak and act. Another thing that makes me angry is being taken advantage of and what makes me the angriest is when people manipulate others. I also get extremely angry when people are harmful to others, either physically or mentally. I also get angry when I feel I am being eliminated."

8. Do you like to work? "Yes, because it is very rewarding to see all of it pay off with hard work and dedication. I like to see my end results."

9. How do you like to spend your leisure time? "I like to spend my leisure time playing video games, going fishing, and going on long bike rides with my dad. I love looking at cheerleaders because they are such beautiful sights. However, my mother is the most beautiful sight I have ever seen."

10. What college classes do you enjoy most in school? "I like any type of science or math classes."

11. What do you find the hardest about working? "Sometimes the hardest thing is working by myself on a task to where I would rather be working with someone but I do get my work done that is required from me."

12. In choosing a career, what are most of your important considerations? "My most important considerations are that I am working for a growing company that will allow growth in the future and that there are room for advancements in my field."

13. What interests you most about any position? "Achieving to my highest goals, as possible."

14. What can you contribute to this organization? "I can contribute a lot to any organization. I am very dedicated and I can get to work on time. I work well with others and communicate well with others, and getting things done. I am always very fair. I can also take constructive criticism."

15. What kind of salary do you have in mind? "I expect to get paid fairly and adequately. My goal is to ultimately be a millionaire."

16. Do you want to get to work on time? "Yes, I get to work early so that I can see what is on the agenda for the day."

17. Can you delegate responsibility? "Yes, I delegate responsibility very well by treating my coworkers the way I would want to be treated."

18. What makes you feel the saddest? "As I was growing up, I felt I was eliminated by others in doing many things they were doing. I felt people just did not want to include me nor wanted me around. They did not want to learn about my situation nor be bothered with it. I felt this happened in most every aspect of my life."

19. What makes you the happiest? "To see all of my wonderful progress, as I excel in many areas, when given the chance. Seeing my parents smiling and happy because today, I have much more knowledge on how extremely hard they worked, to get me where I am today. And as they continue to do this for me, still today. I love you Mom and Dad! Thank you for never giving up on me."

20. How do you feel about autistic people in the workplace? In my opinion, I believe autistic workers are very dedicated, very focused on their tasks and are very reliable workers, like myself. Some autistic

people may need a more structured and routine lifestyle.

21. Is there anything else you would like to add? "Yes, please check out my website at mattsautismjourney.org. Thank you!"

Chapter 4

DAN Treatments

We first heard about DAN (Defeat Autism Now) when Matthew was fifteen years old. My mother found a video online and e-mailed it to us, and we began researching the subject. The closest DAN doctor we found was about two and a half hours away. We were adamant about meeting with this doctor so that we could have some normalcy in our lives, but we really had no idea what we were getting ourselves into.

The cost and rigorous schedule of the DAN treatment was unreal. The DAN doctor did a nutritional and weight analysis and a dietary elimination test, and the doctor looked at genomic variations. I had to devote hours and hours of time to driving back and forth to the clinic and thousands and thousands of dollars to various vitamins, hyperbaric treatments, and blood, urine, and stool testing.

One particular week we lived out of a hotel so Matthew could have several hour-long hyperbaric treatments per day. Matthew didn't mind the hyperbaric chamber at all; he actually liked it. He would sit in there and do homework, play his handheld video games, watch television on his portable TV, study Spell Bowl words, or even just sleep.

The hyperbaric chamber helped Matthew. It provided 100 percent pure oxygen to his brain. We learned that this is a therapy in which pressure is increased in an attempt to boost the amount of oxygen in the brain. Matthew breathed in extra oxygen when he was inside this pressurized chamber. We also learned the pressure helps reduce inflammation to the brain's region that controls speech, cognitive skills, and motor skills to improve the ability to function and concentrate. It improved his understanding. He was less irritable and more responsive when spoken to. He had more eye contact and was more sociable. This helped increase his functioning ability greatly for all those many reasons. He was very calm and content inside the chamber.

Unfortunately, our insurance did not cover any of the cost, because the company said there was not enough significant research about autism at that time to back it up and that the treatment was considered experimental. We fought with the insurance company for almost four years. About two years into it, we contacted a lawyer, and had been working with that lawyer to fight the insurance company. After fighting for a long time to have our insurance company help pay for this autism treatment, the lawsuit ended, and not in our favor. We spent almost $45,000 on this treatment. We of course had to charge most of it; we did not have that amount of money readily available to us.

We just wanted to help Matthew live an independent and productive life, and my husband and I would do whatever it took to ensure this, even if it means paying $45,000 plus interest for the DAN treatment. When I think about it, I get very angry. Why should I have to pay that mass amount of money for my child, when most people with children without disabilities get it for free? This is very disheartening to my husband and I, because we have noticed a significant difference in Matthew since the treatment.

The DAN treatment even relieved the chronic ear infections that plagued Matthew throughout his childhood. From infancy to about the age of sixteen, Matthew would get at least five ear infections a year. Since he was always having ear infections, he was continually taking antibiotics, and it was a great concern for my husband and me. Some people would ask me why Matthew was always getting ear infections. I had already asked the pediatrician about this, and he said some people are more susceptible to certain illnesses, but that Matthew would eventually outgrow them.

The pediatrician also advised us to try to keep Matthew's fingers out of his mouth. Most of the time he would be somewhere touching things that could possibly and most likely did have germs, and then, without washing his hands, he would put is fingers in his mouth, mainly to chew on his nails. It was no surprise to us that he got sick. We constantly—and I mean *constantly*—had to remind him to keep his fingers out of his mouth. We decided to seek the advice of an ear, nose, and throat specialist, and this doctor suggested putting tubes in his ears. Matthew had to have the tubes put in his ears three times. The tubes should have come out on their own, but twice Matthew had to have them removed.

At two years old, Matthew got the worst ear infection he has ever had. His fever skyrocketed so high, so quickly, that he ended up having a seizure. And of course, it was in the middle of the night. My husband immediately called an ambulance, and my motherly instinct told me to grab on to Matthew's tongue. He was biting so hard on my fingers, although I was so scared I did not even notice the pain. This was the first time I really thought I was going to lose my son. I just kept praying and praying.

The paramedics and the doctor both said I should have not have held on to his tongue because he could have bitten my fingers off. I did not care about that. I was only concerned about Matthew, and I would have gladly lost my fingers to save my son's life. I was only doing what my instincts were telling me to do as a mother, to help my son at this time. I did and will continue to do whatever it takes to protect my son.

It seemed like we were constantly at the pediatrician. Matthew always seemed to be sick, and it just did not seem normal to my husband and I. Something was wrong. I could feel it in my gut. But what was it? I thought maybe this was happening because he liked to chew or bite on things—whether a shirt, his fingers, or a blanket—and I would constantly have to remind him to keep things out of his mouth. I constantly insisted on him washing his hands.

The ear infections continued until Matthew underwent his DAN treatment program. After he received that treatment, we saw a significant progress in Matthew—increased communication, for one, which was such an exciting experience for us. Something that most parents take for granted was such an extreme miracle for us. Finding the DAN doctor was a blessing, because we were able to help our Matthew get better, and it made a world of difference for him as well as for our lives. My son is a prime example that this treatment does work. He is now twenty-one years old, and I feel like I'm meeting him for the first time in my life.

I asked Matthew to give you his input on the DAN treatment, and this is what he wrote:

> My name is Matthew, and I am the son of Matt and Patricia. I am their only child. With the information that I will provide, I intend to explain to you why I have to live my life free of certain foods. As many foods had to be taken away from my diet because of my autism. How can a person live gluten-free/casein-free today?
>
> We must first know, what is gluten and casein?
>
> Gluten is a protein found in wheat and other grains, including oats, rye, barley, durum (type of wheat) (found in pizza and pasta), Kamut, and spelt, and foods made from those grains. It is also found in food starches, semolina malts, some vinegars, soy-sauce flavoring, artificial colors and hydrolyzed veggie proteins. Casein is also a protein found in milk. This is found in milk, as well as cheese, butter, yogurt, ice cream, and even some bread or margarine. I would like people to understand why I can only eat certain foods. It may even help them understand about me and autism. Some children diagnosed in the early 1990s like me, I was born in 1992, are likely to have gastrointestinal problems, which included constipation, diarrhea, and vomiting, and blocked bowel syndrome.

Trying to eliminate certain foods from my daily eating habits was very hard and stressful for myself and also for my parents. Some people with autism cannot properly digest gluten and casein from peptides (short chains of amino acids) or substances that act like opiates in their bodies. The peptides often alter a person's behavior, perception, and responses to their environment. Some research has shown that peptides trigger an unusual immune-system response in certain people. My DAN doctor found that in my urinary test, to see if my proteins are being digested properly. Medical tests can most likely determine if you have sensitivity or an allergy to gluten, casein, and other foods, such as eggs, nuts, and soybeans. Some DAN doctors specialize in the field of food allergies and may remove one food at a time so they can narrow down what foods are causing the problem.

DAN doctors may investigate nutrition, detoxification, and removal of interfering factors, such as yeast, food allergies, and heavy metals. In my first case when I went to my DAN doctor, they mentioned if I had warts on either hand. I was shocked and my parents were shocked because I have had these warts for quite some time. Before taking me to the DAN doctor to be seen and evaluated, we had no success in removing some warts on my hand that were there for quite some time. My parents used over-the-counter wart medicine, which did not work. I fought and fought with them as I did not like this process at all. My parents then took me to my general practitioner doctor and they used some type of wart-remover compound, which was also unsuccessful. After my DAN doctor started me on the gluten-free, casein-free diet those warts disappeared within a few weeks. How incredible was that? This was due to the elimination of some gluten and protein in my diet. Some DAN doctors may also ask you to remove milk because the body will clean itself of milk/casein the quickest. In my case it took up to six months on a gluten-free casein-free diet for my body to rid itself of all the gluten. This diet is a lot of very hard work and dedication. A person must carefully read all of the labels on the food packages. They must be aware of hidden casein and gluten in the food they eat on a daily basis. Such ingredients like curd, lactates, bran, spices, or certain types of vinegar. A person on the GFCF diet may find it very difficult to give up regular milk; however there are milk substitutes like rice milk, soy, potato, and even almond milk available. These do all have the enriched vitamins in them, some more than regular 2 percent milk which I think most people are drinking these days. Foods that a person with autism can eat on a GFCF (gluten-free casein-free) diet include rice grains, amaranth potato, buckwheat flour, soy, corn, fruits, oil, vegetable beans, tapioca, meat, poultry, fish, shellfish, and sorghum. Some researchers reported that eye contact improved, less constipation and diarrhea and much better social behavior. However in some others, there was little to no noticeable improvements. There was also a removal, in my case, of soy and corn, which also led to similar growth of social interactions. Although the hypothesis may appear "off the wall" in many respects, there are a number of pieces of evidence which seem to support them. Some doctors and nutritionists in the Defeat Autism Now biomedical movement have recommended enzyme supplements to help some patients digest foods that cause problems for them. Such supplements like B6 and B12 with minerals, magnesium, zinc, and essential fatty acids like purified fish oil. The supplements calcium, magnesium, zinc, and vitamin D are especially important for people on gluten-free and casein-free diets to replace the nutrients found in cow's milk. Besides the gluten and foods of other dietary components that could possibly worsen autism symptoms include food preservatives, such as benzoate, nitrates, and monosodium glutamate. These dietary methods must be considered as experimental and no positive results can be promised or claimed for every person diagnosed with the autism spectrum. Let it also be known that this type of treatment is very expensive, depending on the individual and the severity of the disability treatment program they need. My autism treatment consisted of forty hyperbaric-chamber treatments.

A hyperbaric chamber is the process of breathing pure oxygen while the patient is under increased barometric pressure. I was put in a large chamber which I could lay down, watch a TV that was portable, or do homework, sleep, or practice my Spell Bowl words, or play on a handheld video game. I would also like to add that my doctor included in my treatment multiple nutritional vitamin supplements which in my case, I was taking twenty-five vitamins in the morning and twenty-five more vitamins at night along with a nutrient enriched shake. My treatment reached approximately $45,000 for a two-and-a-half-year treatment. As with many parents' medical insurance, most insurance companies do not cover this treatment because I think they feel it is experimental and not enough research to back it up.

With this type of gluten-free, casein-free treatment program, this could last a person upwards from twelve to thirty months for a person on the autism spectrum. I have much knowledge on this, because I was a patient and lived through it all. It was a very difficult experience. My parents help me monitor the foods I eat today. I am very aware of what I should and should not eat. Sometimes my body will even tell me if I have had too much of something, as I just don't feel the way I normally should. Thank goodness the food market has realized there is a need for this type of foods and you can now see them at more stores.

These types of food are very expensive and hopefully now with such a demand for them, the prices can be more affordable for families to purchase and help their special-needs children. Thank you, Matt DeGeyter.

These are questions and answers Matthew got from his DAN doctor:

1. Why does gluten, wheat, and dairy need to be eliminated from an autistic person's diet? "It is relatively common that individuals who are diagnosed on the autism spectrum of disorders may have a sensitivity or allergy to the proteins found in dairy and wheat. Eliminating these proteins from the diet often relieves many of the symptoms associated with the spectrum of autism disorders."

2. Why are the vitamins so important to an autistic person's system? "Children and people on the autism spectrum commonly suffer from disruptions in how they absorb, digest, and utilize nutrients, minerals, and vitamins. Thus, it is important to administer the necessary nutrients to help them restore their health to their fullest potential."

3. How does an autistic person benefit from hyperbaric chamber treatments? "Oxygen is a necessary component to heal tissues including stimulating the brain to heal. Hyperbaric oxygen therapy is administered to help the person's brain build new blood vessels therefore healing brain tissue and helping the person improve their thinking, their eye contact, their social interaction, and help support the healing of tissue that may have been disrupted due to the antibodies produced in response to food allergies and sensitivities."

4. Why are DAN (Defeat Autism Now) doctors so important to autism treatments? "Many doctors get together to share their training and learn treatments to help their patients who are struggling with autism disorders. DAN is a group of doctors who share information, specialized training, and therefore many times they are able to offer patients more specialized treatment."

5. What is your personal opinion on what causes autism? "I think the cause is multifactorial. In susceptible individuals it is sometimes triggered by a combination of genetic factors and environmental exposures at critical stages of development."

6. What is the best treatment for autism today? "The research is clear that the safest, most effective, and preferred method of treatment includes a complex combination of dietary intervention, specific nutraceutical prescriptions, hyperbaric oxygen therapy, and biotransformation therapies."

7. How long does it take to rid a body of gluten? "Individuals will vary, but if they strictly follow a gluten-free diet, the antibodies to gluten should decrease significantly in about one year. However, gluten must continue to be eliminated from the diet permanently to maintain the low antibody response and to maintain the improvements the individual has experienced."

8. What is gluten? "Gluten is a protein found in three grains that we commonly eat: wheat, barley, and rye."

9. Does gluten affect the brain's function? "Yes, in my opinion, it does."

10. Why is there so much testing involved in the treatment? "Laboratory evaluation aids the doctor in supporting how the doctor can safely and effectively administer treatment."

11. What are the effects on the body if an autistic person has too much in their system? "The symptoms can affect any organ in the body so the symptoms are quite variable, but here are several examples: reduced cognitive functions, psoriasis/eczema, anxiety, depression, seizures, reduced immune-system function, joint aches, muscle aches, poor growth, poor tooth development, digestive dysfunctions, constipation, diarrhea, gas, bloating, low thyroid function, irregular heartbeat, and infertility."

12. Are gluten-, wheat-, and casein-free diets easy to maintain? "Most patients who have noticed how much better they feel find the elimination diets are well worth maintaining."

13. Why are certain toxins and chemicals so sensitive to the body of an autistic person? "Many people

with autism spectrum disorders have experienced the combination of predisposing genetics that make it difficult for them to eliminate environmental toxins with an increased exposure at an early stage of development, which results in the expression of symptoms that are commonly referred to as 'autism.'"

14. Why do certain foods have such an adverse effect on people with autism? "They often have a condition called intestinal hyper permeability that makes them more susceptible to developing adverse reactions to multiple foods."

15. Is there a possibility of environmental factors that could also have triggered autism? "Yes, there is a possibility of environmental factors that could also have been a contributing factor to the autism epidemic we are seeing today."

All of Matthew's special needs were and still are out-of-pocket expenses for my husband and I. We never, ever received any financial help from the insurance company, the state, or any governmental office for our child's disability. By now, we hope that all special-needs children and their parents are getting the financial assistance they so desperately need to improve their special child's quality of life, and whatever care they may need. It is such a strain and an extreme nightmare to not have this much-needed help.

In our opinion, having to be in so much financial debt just because you want to help your special-needs child is pathetically unfair. It is already difficult enough for us parents to have a child with a disability, but then to add the financial burden on top of that, is incomprehensible. Please, start helping these special children with disabilities and their families, in every area. They so desperately need the help.

I need to emphasize that today the autism still exists, as there is no cure. We still endure times of trouble in certain areas and I still work diligently toward his success. However, my son is a prime example that an autistic child can grow and prosper in a world that is unfamiliar to them, overcome many obstacles, and become successful in our world.

In my opinion early intervention is very essential for the growth of any child diagnosed with autism. As in our case, our son was diagnosed at the age of three years old, however in today's studies autism can be diagnosed at a much earlier age. There are many more options for dealing and surviving the autism diagnosis today, then when we found out about our son's autism in the early 1990's. We were told that autism is known for being more prevalent in boy than in girls. As a mother of an autistic child, I believe there just has to be more research to determine why this happens and we must gain more recognition on what causes autism. Could environmental factors be attributed to autism in today's world? This question is still unanswered for us. I think it is imperative that education of autism is very important for all and any family members to educate themselves on autism, so they all could have a better understanding of the parents and the autistic child, that is in their family. In my opinion, I truly believe all of society should also educate themselves as well, as they may eventually come in contact with a very special person who has autism.

Chapter 5

Family and Friends

If it wasn't for the love of both of our families and many friends, we couldn't have raised such an amazing son. We are so grateful for all their support, care, and love. Here are some stories and experiences those who love or worked with Matthew have shared about our special son.

First, unfortunately my husband's parents have both passed away; I want to say something on their behalf. They loved Matthew very much and were so happy to have him in their life. Matt's father, Morris, would always have tears in his eyes whenever he was with Matthew, no matter what they were doing together, whether it was watching the trains or playing a game. Ginny (Virginia) was such a wonderful grandmother. Matthew always enjoyed his time with her. I know he misses and loves them both very much.

Morris and Virginia DeGeyter

Grandma and Grandpa DeGeyter

Gaylord "Buzz" and Josephine Powell
Grandma and Grandpa Powell

I would watch my daughter Patricia cry and say, "Mom, my Matthew never says he loves me or hugs me. If only one day he would come to me and show me he loves me." So many years later, Matthew shows his mom how much he really loves her (all the time). I remember how much his Grandpa Powell would assist Matthew on our computer during many of his early years; then at one point, Matthew would have his own computer. Matthew always loved to visit me and spend the night. Now I know he is ready to be an adult. He doesn't want to spend the night like he used to.

Where we lived we had a swing on our porch. When Matthew was over and his parents were working, we would spend hours swinging. Sometimes he would take his nap while I sat beside him, and when he awoke, we would have lunch and then go back to the swing and watch the trains go by at a distance. These are just a few things I remember about one of my sweet grandbabies. I love you, Matthew. May God be with you always and forever.

Love, Grandma Powell.

Gaylord "Buzz" Powell
Matthew's grandfather (now deceased)

Matthew was about three years old and visiting with Grandma and Grandpa Powell. I took Matthew for a walk. The street was two blocks long. There was a certain place where Matthew would turn around, but it was not the end of the block. How he made that decision was a mystery to me. He would not allow any variation from his pattern. I could not induce him to turn in more interesting directions, just up and down and turn at the same spots. All of the homes in my subdivision looked essentially the same—same exteriors, same position on the lot, same driveway, and same mailboxes. This could be confusing to any three-year-old. However, when Matthew was tired and wanted to quit walking, he knew exactly which house was his grandparents' without any help from me.

Flash forward one year. Matthew went for another walk with me, but this time I tried a little experiment. When I came to Matthew's turnaround point, I continued to walk without looking at Matthew. Out of the corner of my eye, I could see Matthew hesitating, wanting to turn, but I kept walking. After a short hesitation, Matthew continued to follow me. I thought, *Aha! Matthew's parents are making progress getting him to respond to others.* Matthew allowed me to lead him down to the river's edge, and there I would find rocks and show him how to make a splash by throwing them into the water. Matthew loved that game.

Aunt Meffy Gamache

I helped my sister watch Matthew from time to time when he was small (I believe around four years old) and she was working. Trisha used to say to me, "I never hear my son say 'I love you, Mom.'" I know this broke her heart. One day when she was at work and I was watching her son, I said to myself, "I need to make this happen for her." So we listened to a music CD of *The Music Man*. I realized that Matthew was really enjoying it, especially the song "Marian the Librarian." We danced and marched around the house, singing it all day (I do mean *all day*). We played this particular song over and over and over again. Each time at the end of the song, I looked at Matthew and showed him a picture of his mom and I said, "I love you, Mom." He in turn repeated it out loud. We practiced it all day long, so when she came to pick her son up, I said "I have a special surprise for you." So we then turned the song on and marched and danced to it, and at the end of the song he said by himself in a very soft, sweet voice, "I love you, Mom." I was so proud of him, and it made his mama cry. She gave him the biggest hug with tears in her eyes, and she said, "I love you too, son, so much." She thanked me and asked how in the world I did it. I told her we practiced on it all day and we were going to have it happen . . . and that we did.

I have to say I am very proud of my nephew Matthew. He has come such a long way, and each year he is smarter and more handsome. He is very polite and loving, and I know when I walk through their door I will be greeted with a big, fat hug from him. I believe strongly he wouldn't be where he is today if it was not for his loving parents who fought for him and raised him without limits. Not only am I proud of my nephew, I am also very proud of my sister and her husband. I realize this is a hard journey and struggle, but they always got through it. They have made Boonsey (Matthew) what he is today: a fine young man with a great future. He will go far. I love them all.

Love, Aunt Meffy.

Aunt Cecilia Brendel

Dear Matthew,

I want to tell you a few things about your mom and dad. I would like to start with your mother, my sister, that I am closest in age to. When your mom was a little girl she used to play school and had lots of pretend students. How she loves children so much, that's all she ever wanted was to have lots of them of her own and she also wanted to be a teacher when she got older. As a child, I would be amazed at how much paper your mom would use to teach all of these pretend children math, reading, art etc. It was a daily retreat for her to escape and love all the little children in her own way. Secretly, I would be impressed since I was not good in school.

As your mother got older she was called to help your grandma and grandpa to work at the Italian restaurant they owned. She managed this for the entire time it was open. When it came time for your grandparents to sell the restaurant, they asked her if she would be interested in it. Your mother declined this because all she ever wanted was to fill her dreams of getting married and having lots of children to love.

A few years later she did marry your father Matthew Sr. It was the beginning of a beautiful dream come true. A year after their marriage your mother and father gave birth to you. What a beautiful baby boy, Matthew. As you got older your parents noticed that you did not seem to respond when they would call your name. By the age of three, they became increasingly worried that something might be hindering your hearing. At the age of three your speech was of a babbling stage and was of its own degree. No notable words were being used and this really is what got your parents to proceed with the testing to see if you had anything that was able to help your mom and dad understand the meaning behind it all.

After getting the diagnosis of you being autistic, this was very upsetting because of the unknown. With years of patience and love for you they struggled with teachers year after year for the help that they wanted for you, their son. Your mother fought for you and went from a very shy little girl to this mighty warrior with a voice that had the authority of God behind her! As an observer, I was amazed at how God can use anyone for his work! Even with the meekest, shy and most unlikely persons. Yes, your mother and father became such advocates for you because at that time in history, autism was barely being studied by scientist. So it was not quite understood by many people in the school system or any where!

Your mother and father saw the beauty and powerful potential that you had as an individual and they wanted every possible normal way of growth for you. This society does not seem to cater to the poor and humble such as your parents, this world caters to the wealthy. Society will give to anyone who has money but to those who have not, they sneer at you and balk at the inconvenience that is given. Many times your parents endured dirty looks from strangers and no one wanting to help out. Even their own marriage and other relationships had its struggles to keep the love intact.

This did not stop your loving parents. You would be so proud to remember that every week they helped you with studies showed you how to communicate, how to love and how to speak for yourself. So much was very disheartening to them, but you, my good man, were never a burden. You were their whole life, you were their source of love and you were their inspiration. You are now a very wonderful grown man with dreams of your own. These dreams are possible by the grace of God and never underestimate the power behind a very small person who became a very big voice in the name of God, your mother and father.

One last note; your mother, Patricia, once thought she was going to be a teacher and teach lots of children. But, I believe God had a different class room in mind for her. The class room would be large and would contain lots of God's children, the parents of all autistic children throughout the world. To help them with the struggles they will go through and support them in their times of distress and to never, ever give up. She will indeed be a teacher and advocate for all autistic children and their parents. We all are so very proud of you and your parents. If it was not for the patience and love they had, we would not have such a great advocate, not to mention, a wonderful man, you, to give all the world hope for anyone to have dreams to come true.

My loving sister Patricia and her wonderful husband Matt have been exceptional parents to their son Matthew. They have had years of being Matthew's voice teaching him, supporting him, and standing up for him by being his voice for all his life so far. Now that Matthew has grown into this amazing responsible young man that can hold a stable job, earn his own income, study for himself and even driving a car. As I see Matthew and Patricia allowing their son to speak for himself, learn for himself and to make decisions for himself, this struggle has been accomplished. I am sure it was a long time effort to break away from since they had been his voice for so long. But with the grace of god and their wisdom they have found, Matthew has become a very successful man that can live in society and function on his own and be productive and wise as his parents are.

I love you Aunt Cecilia Brendel

Aunt Laurie Powell

Matthew was blessed to have a mother and father who have shown fierce belief in the can-dos versus the can't-dos. As one of the aunts of Matthew and the mother of a special-needs child myself, I know that, regardless of our determination as parents, the real determination must come from the person themselves. Matthew has amazed all of us by meeting each challenge head-on. We are so proud of Matthew. His story can be a true inspiration to anyone who has a special-needs person in their life.

Mr. Dave Hamrick
(Special friend of the family with autism)

One of my best experiences with Matthew was hearing him recite the names of the US presidents in chronological order and hearing him spell very difficult words. These days I have been impressed to see that he has successfully graduated high school and now is in college to get his future ready in starting his career choice. Even though he has autism, he has been able to overcome many of its challenges through a very caring family and helpful support systems in place.

Aunt Rita Bagnall

There was a time I was in the bank waiting in line with Matthew when he was about five years old. As we were waiting, he began to read all the advertising on the walls in the bank out loud. All the customers turned around and watched him. They asked how old he was and said they could not believe he could read all that. I was very proud.

Love, Aunt Rita

Aunt Diana Callihan

My memories as Matthew's aunt are most joyous ones. Although, I have seen my sister Trisha and my brother-in-law Matt struggling many times in frustration. Why they have been chosen to raise an autistic child I will touch on later in my story. I remember when Matthew was a small child; about five or six, I gave him trading cards of the presidents and the presidents' wives. These cards had the complete history of each president, the times they were in office, when they were born, who they were married to, and when they died. I was so amazed Matthew was absorbed so deeply into our American History of presidents.

Kennedy born May 29, 1917, in Brookline Massachusetts, died November 22, 1963." And not only that, he would go on and on about this president until you finally had to say "Matthew, Matthew what about the sixteenth president?" Matthew's bedroom walls became filled with pictures of presidents and more.

Matthew loved learning, and the best part was that it stayed in his brilliant mind. Like most of us without autism, if we don't use it, we lose it. This young man's brilliant mind came at such an early age from reading a telephone book, knowing all the presidents' histories, sports, and spelling. I couldn't be more amazed as to how intelligent he became. When Matthew was in high school, he was in Spell Bowl competitions—spelling words perfectly that even young doctors and lawyers can't spell. Matthew and his team had won these competitions and even went so far as to win three state championships in his four-year Spell Bowl career.

Matthew is a winner in more ways than I can even place into words. Matthew shows so much love towards his parents now. Matthew loves and idolizes his mother and father. He is deeply affectionate, and I love this about Matthew. Most parents who have teenagers have to deal with conflicts and other aspects in raising a teenager. I very much admire Matthew's parents for being able to handle these things along with autism.

Matthew has a beautiful soul; he is loving, innocent, and a beautiful gift from God. I'm deeply and sincerely proud of my nephew Matthew, and I do believe God knows what he does when he has us face autism in our family. This is where I give my dear, sweet sister Trisha and my wonderfully supportive brother-in-law credit for my nephew's talents, abilities, and beautiful soul. It is the strength of a strong and faithful family to stay together and face the challenges most of us are frightened to deal with. Trisha and Matt are a prime example of God's holy presence when we need him. To raise a child with autism is to know you cannot do it all alone. You need and must have support from your family, your faith, and God. I love Matthew.

Love, Aunt Diana Marie.

Uncle Dan Powell
(Late Aunt Mary Powell)

I am so very proud of Trisha and Matt, and of course little Matt. Without the love, devotion, and dedication of Trisha and Matt, Matthew would not be leading such a fulfilled life and would not be where he is today. It is their undying fight for their son that made him the extraordinary young man he is now. A young man we are all so proud of. I know that my late wife, Mary, shared something special with Matthew. I'm not sure what, but I know she loved him. I remember her talking with me about Matthew and saying she knew, somehow, inexplicably, that their son would excel. Mary loved him. We all do. Love, Uncle Danny and Aunt Mary.

Cousin Sarah Lambdin

Some of my fondest memories of Matthew involve taking him on walks in his red wagon when he lived on Hubbard Street. We would walk down the block and sometimes were lucky enough to see a train go by. I remember he was always very calm and content taking this walk, and very enthralled by the trains. A lot of times he would fall asleep on the walk, but if he didn't fall asleep and wasn't interested in going home, he would get very upset when we turned the corner to go back to their house, so we would have to go around the block a few more times. I love you, Matthew.

Love, Cousin Sarah.

Aunt Mary Grace Stephens

I can say that Matthew is a fine example of a kind, gentle human being who is so loved by his parents who have fought long and hard for his happiness. My two sons adore Matthew and love spending time with him. You need that love and support of family when raising a special-needs child.

Love, Aunt Mary Grace.

Aunt Kathy Koen

The transformation of Matthew's demeanor has been amazing over the past few years. He has actually become a young man who now realizes that the universe consists of love by and for other people. Matthew is conscious of others' feelings, and this never was the case before his parents were able to provide him with the medical treatment he needed to control his autism.

The first indication that I had that something might be wrong with little Matthew was when we were all around the kitchen table singing happy birthday to Matt when he was two. The singing was so unpleasant to his ears that he just kept screaming and screaming. He did not enjoy this loud attention. I also remember when he came to visit my home in Michigan several years ago. He enjoyed the first day, but after that he was anxious to get back to his familiar routine at home and kept chanting, "I don't want to go back to: and he would mention my home address. Well, at least he memorized my address, and I joke about it with him from time to time.

As Matthew has gotten a little older, he has become more aware of having aunts and uncles. He would come up and give us a greeting hug. Finally, I got a hug and kiss from Matthew. As he matured, I would send him greeting cards and write in some silly math or word puzzles. I hope he enjoyed playing those puzzles as much as I did writing them in for him. Matthew has so much potential, and it will be exciting to see what he does with his life. I say he will be great.

Uncle Sam Powell

What can I say about Matthew? As his uncle and a teacher, I am very proud to call him my nephew. He is an inspiration to anyone who has battled adversity. His success as a team Spell Bowl state champion and achievements of a high-school graduate and a college student has impressed everyone who has gotten to know him. Matthew's accomplishments should be a lesson to all of us that yes, we can reach our goals regardless of what challenges we may face. He is a fine young man, and his parents, Patricia and Matthew Sr., have done a great job raising him and should feel very proud of their accomplishments.

Matthew has an entire life ahead of him and over time, I am very confident that he will make positive contributions to our world. Your family loves you, Matthew, and we are praying that you continue to grow in a positive direction

Aunt Carrie Durrett

I am Aunt Carrie to Matthew. His presence in our huge family, of 10 siblings on his fathers side and 11 siblings on his mother's side, has made Matthew one much loved person. As a baby he was consoled and held in our arms, all of trying to soothe or recognize his needs. Since his roots were from a Belgian and Italian family we just figured he was showing us how stubborn he could be!!!

When Matt was diagnosed with autism, it became an odyssey of love and understanding. His parents stepped right up learning everything about autism. They had first-hand knowledge on how to deal with Matthew, because they lived it. The rest of us watched in awe at his accomplishments over the years. I would scratch my head and realize that he was smarter than me!!!

Getting those hugs and kisses from Matthew was the best feeling deep down in my heart. I was the one who is truly blessed. For to engage in a conversation with Matt was a little hard times, I know that he always had something on his mind. He always was having somewhere to go or somewhere to do something. He was a busy little boy!!!

And now he is a busy young man. The world is his oyster in our Sea of Life. Just like the rest of us with decisions and opportunities. His parents raised a wonderful person. Can't wait to see what he's up to next.

Cousin Audrey DeGeyter

The only time I normally see Matthew is when the holidays roll around, and when I do he is a joy. He is so polite and so caring! Always giving hugs and asking me how I am. He loves to play with our little cousins, and it is so fun watching them. I love my cousin Matthew.

Cousin James Bishop

Matthew has grown up to become a fine young gentleman, brilliant and smart, admittedly a bit young at heart. He has always been very respectful and kind. Also, seems to have gotten some of his father's handsome looks. He is and will always be my cousin.

Cousin Olivia Stuber

I haven't really grown up around Matthew, so I have limited knowledge about his everyday life, but what I do know from the e-mails is that he is a bright guy, and it sure is amazing that he has been in the local newspaper! Growing up I really had only seen him a handful of times, and a couple of those times were probably around Christmas, and that means a lot of family around. And I have to admit even I have had and still have a hard time finding things to talk about with my family that I never really, really got to know because of living so far away from everyone. So it is no wonder that one of the times I remember Matthew is at four or five years old at my uncle's house for Christmas; he just seemed overwhelmed and upset and you, Aunt Trisha, were there trying to talk to him and comfort him next to the Christmas tree. Little did you all know I was overwhelmed in those social situations too! I could only imagine how he felt.

Now, I know I have probably seen him in between four and five years old and being a teenager, but the other times that stick out in my mind when I was around Matthew was I think at our Grandma DeGeyter's funeral, when Matthew was completely different. Not scared, not screaming, shaking, or yelling. He was a lot older and a preteen or teenager. My memories of Matthew are that he is very loving, gives hugs, and loves telling us about his spelling competitions. I thought it was going to be awkward, but it wasn't. I wasn't sure how he was going to react before I started the conversation, but immediately it was fine, my shyness of him went away. He is a super cool dude.

Uncle Mark and Aunt Sheila DeGeyter

One night we were down in Mishawaka visiting Grandpa Moose and Grandma Ginny DeGeyter and decided to stop by to see Matt, Trisha, and Matthew. He was doing homework in the living room on the coffee table. Matt and Trisha were ready to pull their hair out because they couldn't seem to help Matthew understand the subjects he was working on. I started talking to Matthew about what he was working on, and we were able to finish his homework painlessly. Sheila started to help him with the next subject he had homework in, and they were able to finish without too much trouble. Matt and Trisha were so happy we had stopped by. We explained to them it wasn't that we are so smart but that sometimes kids need to look at things in a different way and hear it from someone other than their parents.

Another time we remember so clearly is when we again had come to Matt and Trisha's house and they told us about how Matthew could tell you the day of the week that your birthday was on in the future. We thought that maybe Matt was playing a trick on us, but Matthew had been studying the calendar with the months and dates on the computer. Matt asked us our birthdays, and Matthew told us the day of the week it was on in that year. We were amazed—he didn't get any wrong.

He would come to our house to spend the night when Matt and Trisha would go out for their wedding anniversary. He was always good for us, never cried for his dad and mom. One morning we were just getting ready to eat breakfast and his parents came. We told them to "go away," because we weren't ready for them to come get him.

We are so proud of Matthew and his parents and how far they all have come. If it wasn't for their love and commitment to him, he would not be where is today. Impressed, graduating from high school, being a team state champion in Spell Bowl, driving a car, taking college classes, and having a job. Remarkable!

Uncle Steve Gamache

Let's see, I can recall some very interesting things about Matthew. Taking him and Robbie (my son) on a trip to McDonald's, we stopped to get something to eat, and I gave everyone their meal. I handed Robbie his Happy Meal and then handed Matthew his—mistake. I think Meffy said he was terrified of the bag, he started screaming, and once we took everything out of the bag, Matthew was just fine; he would not touch the bag. I came home from work and went to the refrigerator to get something cool to drink and noticed all the eggs had holes in them. I asked Meffy what happened—did someone get mad at the eggs or something? She came to look and said, "That little stinker Matthew was here today and must have gotten to the eggs." So guess what we had for dinner: about a dozen scrambled eggs. I thought maybe he just hated eggs.

Now, he is heading over to the bread. This I knew he loved. He will sit and eat a whole loaf of bread by himself. Hide the steaks, Matthew is coming over . . . LOL. All kidding aside, from the time he was born to the present day, I have watched Matthew grow up to be a fine young man. I am so proud of him and all the accomplishments: his Spell Bowl championship he and his team won for his high school, his graduation, and his attendance of a community college student to become a sports writer or journalist. But whatever Matthew does, he does with his whole heart in it. I am proud to be his Uncle Steve.

Cousin Stevie Charlie Gamache

My name is Steve, I am Matt's cousin. We've grown up together, and it's been a journey for the both of us. He's a very intelligent young man for his age with big goals in mind. He's going places. A shining example of patience and dedication from his parents, for sure. I believe I share a very special relationship with Matt. We understand each other.

When I think of Matt, a few memories instantly come to mind. I remember the time he was in the hospital after he had an accident with a cup of hot coffee. My mom and I had just arrived at his room at the hospital, and my aunt Trish told Matt that my mom had come to visit. He seemed happy, but didn't show it in a big way. Trish had mentioned I was there, and his eyes got big! He was smiling, just so excited I had come to visit.

I also remember all the time we spent outside in the backyard. We would always have a good time with each other. Or the drives I would take with Matt to try and share my love of music with him, showing him new bands, different genres, or just what I was interested in at the time.

Matt is my cousin, and my friend. If he ever needed anything, I am sure he knows I am there for him as I know he is there for me. As I mentioned, we have a very special relationship. And I wouldn't trade the times I've spent with him for anything in the world.

Cheers buddy.

Cousin Charles Robert Gamache

My name is Robert. I am Matthew's cousin. Matthew and I have been friends for a long time. I used to love spending the night with him because we had fun all night. Even though we were supposed to go to bed, we wanted to stay up all night. Matthew is very smart, and he can always keep a smile on your face. If you are having the worst day of your life, he can bring a smile to your face. He's my cousin and always will be, no matter what happens.

Uncle Mike Brendel

Matt is an amazing person. Intense in his mission, focused on the task, and free in spirit. I remember one visit where he had a keen interest in the telephone book. He was soaking in the names, looking for patterns, synthesizing connections—like candy for the mind. But what struck me the most is that I did the same sort of thing as a kid. Matt reminds me of me! It's always a pleasure to visit with Matt, and I look forward to watching him grow. Matt's parents have done an outstanding job nurturing his unique gifts and abilities. He is a bright young man with an exciting journey ahead of him. I'm glad he is part of my world!

Cousin Rebecca Eaker

Here's my experience: I remember my first time interacting with Matthew. He was a little one—probably four or five years old. We were celebrating our grandparents' wedding anniversary, and there were lots of people around. I noticed he was playing underneath one of the tables, alone and with a calculator. I knew of his diagnosis at that point and I was in college, studying psychology. So I had a minimal understanding of children with autism.

When I first went to talk to him, he would not look at me. He was just typing in his calculator. I said hi and he remained quiet, continuing to avoid eye contact with me. I knew this was normal and decided to see if I could connect with him anyway. I got down on the floor with him, the table legs between us. He noticed I was there and scooted a little away from me, but not completely. I asked him if I could see his calculator. After a few seconds, he showed it to me, still not looking up. I asked him if he could count numbers for me. I started with something easy and asked him to add 2 and 2. I watched him type it in and the screen showed 4. He lifted the calculator to show me the answer. We had connected. He and I spent several minutes under the table, adding numbers on the calculator. The longer we were there, the more comfortable he became. I even got to see his pretty brown eyes a few times! He continued to add some numbers for me and would show me time.

At one point the party guests had gathered to watch a video of pictures of our grandparents, and I walked over to the crowd. Matthew followed me, keeping his distance, but definitely *with* me. I remember feeling a sense of connectedness with him that was very different than any of the other children. Obviously, the way we connected *was* different, but I knew there was a little connection there! It is pretty neat how Matthew has grown into such a smart and mature young man!

Aunt Tina Dunwoody

I remember when Matthew Mark was bitten by a neighborhood dog . . . he became very terrified to be around any dogs. Unfortunately, several of his relatives have dogs: we have a Labrador retriever and a beagle mix. When Matthew would come over to our home, we would have to put our dogs in another room (which they did not like at all). Matthew would slowly come into the house, very cautiously, looking for the dogs, making sure they wouldn't come close to him. This went on for several months, but we didn't give up. We felt that if Matthew knew that not every dog might hurt him, he wouldn't be so nervous around them. We slowly got him to allow the dogs to smell his pant leg or lick his hand, but the dog had to be held back by us so Matthew would feel safe. He would feed my brothers' dog while it was in its cage. We gradually got him to allow the dogs to get closer to him, but still the dog had to be held back by its owner. After months of this caution, somehow, some way, Matthew realized that the dogs were his friends and he didn't have to be afraid of them. Today, he can be found lying on the floor next to the dog(s), petting them and talking to them. What a beautiful sight!

Karl Kerrn
(Special family friend)

I have known Matthew for all his life. He has always impressed me on his knowledge of spelling very difficult words. His ability to remember certain things and his intelligence about sports is just amazing. I am very proud of Matt and wish him the very best in life and whatever he chooses for his career. His parents are to be commended on the excellent job that have accomplished with raising this very special young man.

Keely Tobar
(Special family friend)

Matthew is such a wonderful, kind, and caring young man. I am honored to have met him. I did not know much about autism until I met Matthew. All of his accomplishments amaze me, and I know he will go far in life. I look forward to watching him grow and become very successful. Best wishes Matthew and God bless you!

Mrs. Melin
(Matthew's program assistant)

I am a program assistant that works with special-needs children who are included in the classroom. I have had the privilege of working with Matthew for five years, from first grade through fifth grade.

Matthew demonstrated his flexibility early on when his family moved to a new house. Unbeknownst to his parents, this move meant a change in schools. Mom was very worried, but Matthew took it all in stride!

Of course there were struggles at the new school as it would be with any child with autism. I wrote many social stories dealing with such things as cooperation, going to specials, eating in the lunchroom, and even being kind to horses (for Reins of Life).

Another struggle typical of children with autism is the inability to tell someone how they feel. One day I could tell Matthew did not feel well, though he was not able to tell me. As we were walking down the hall (I was carrying a wastebasket)—out "it" came! Good thing I had quick reflexes!

Along with struggles there were many proud moments. Matthew had excellent memorization skills and was an expert speller. He made the Spell Bowl team, much to the surprise of some, but not to me. Fast forward to high school. What fun it was for me to watch, with his family, as seventeen-year-old Matthew spelled every difficult word correctly.

Another proud time was when Matthew was in fifth grade. All fifth-graders go to camp, spending two nights away from home. I also went to camp as his program assistant. I had a blast and he did just fine. This change in schedule did not bother him.

Matthew has been successful for many reasons. As his program assistant I was pretty tough on him. I expected a lot out of him—and got it. But more importantly, Matthew has two parents who love and support him and who support each other. This makes all the difference. Sure, Matthew "follows the beat of a different drummer," but his beat is beautiful. Thanks, Trisha and Matt, for trusting me with your son.

Mr. DeKever

(Matthew's Spell Bowl Coach)

One of the greatest experiences I have had in my eighteen years of coaching Spell Bowl was watching Matt's growth and achievement on our team. When Matt was a freshman and sophomore he struggled greatly with just the social and organizational aspects of being on the team, but as a junior and senior, he transformed into a highly capable team member and fully came into his own as a speller.

We relied on his consistent perfect scores, and Matt was a big part of our offense. Seeing him get a perfect score in the state finals was a memorable victory at a personal level and not just because it helped us win a state championship. I was always impressed by how much Spell Bowl meant and still means to Matt, how dedicated and enthusiastic he was.

One of the lasting images I have of Matt's Spell Bowl years is how he would thrust his arm straight up after a correct spelling; I even used him as a model to others for how to show we had spelled correctly. Another great moment is a picture I have of Matt as we rode home on the bus after Matt's senior state championship. In it, Matt has this wonderful smile of pride and satisfaction, which perfectly represents his Spell Bowl achievement. It's one of my favorite Spell Bowl pictures.

Aunt Mary Mantese

Patricia is a strong and sensitive young woman. She works hard for the love of her son. She sent him to college and demands the best for him. She is a pillar of strength for her son, Matthew, whom we all love. I had the opportunity to visit my sister at her home in Indiana. I was looking forward to the visit, and having time to talk to my nieces and nephews. When I arrived at my sister's home, I noticed on the front door of her refrigerator was a small sticker that said, "I love an autistic child". I was very moved by the sticker, and I asked my sister, who gave her the sticker. My sister said that it was her daughter Patricia, whose son Matthew is autistic. I was very proud to be part of the family. Patricia was just like her Mom. She loves her child with her whole heart. That is why Matthew has excelled. He has a Mom that believes in him.

Love, Aunt Mary

The Colbert Family
(Special family friends)

I am so proud of you Trish. Matthew has grown so much since we moved here. He would often come into our house and help himself to a drink or whatever he wanted to eat. If there was company here he still came in and opened the refrigerator and took out a can of pop. People would always comment to us, who is that? We would say he's family- That's Matthew. I remember when he started to notice the girls. There were so many memories with him I just have to mention when he got injured by a dog and refused to go outside. My son Kevin refused to give up on him, until he left that house and came outside to play. I cried when I heard that my son got him to come out and play. We love you guys so much. I better stop because I will be writing a book on how great you and your husband are as parents. When my niece had her son and he was diagnosed to be autistic, I told her about you and it gave her hope. I told you this is your calling to help others. God Bless you and I am waiting for my copy. (Signed, of course).

The Colbert Family

Matthew's Father

Only a father could feel this way about his son. Matthew, I'm so proud of you and all you have conquered in your life so far. Please continue to do your best. Keep in mind that nothing is out of your reach, if you want it bad enough. You have made your mother and I *very proud of you*. Keep up the great job you have done and undoubtedly will continue to do so. You continue to always amaze me with all your accomplishments. I love you son.

Love, Dad.

Matthew's Mother

I love you, my Matthew. I am so grateful to have you as my son. You are my very special handsome son. I love you so very much. How do you suppose God blessed me to have you as my very own special child? I honor you, respect you, I have so much love for you, and I care deeply for you. I am so very proud of you. Keep up the great work and always remember your education. You are always continually shining your love into my life. My world is a better place because of you and I will always be forever thankful to you for that. I see the best in you and all the joy you have brought into my life. Continue to work hard and enjoy seeing more and more of what you can and have accomplished in life so far. You will go far in life, there is no doubt. You are a true inspiration, and I admire you greatly. Please always remember, no star is out of reach. I love you, my dear son! God bless you, my darling! You are my son! I love you so very much.

Love, your mother.

Matthew and Patrica DeGeyter
Matthew's Parents

About the Author

My name is Patricia DeGeyter, and I am a mother of an autistic child, my special son, Matthew. I was raised by my mother's Italian influence into a catholic family of eleven children. I lived with my mother and father along with my five brothers and 5 sisters. Growing up I always wanted to be a teacher. Shortly after graduating high school, my parents had bought a small Italian restaurant, which I worked at for approximately nine years. While working at my parent's restaurant, I also attended college for a few years and studied restaurant management. My husband proposed to me, at my parent's restaurant. I then got married, and also anxiously wanting a child. My story is based on my experience raising an autistic child that I will share and make awareness. After learning of my son's autism diagnosis, autism had become my career. I will take you on a journey about my life in raising my special child, from the earliest stages up until now. I will illustrate my struggles and hardships in getting through it all, and the ending results of having such an amazing autistic son, who has overcome many very difficult obstacles in his life. Today, I feel I am meeting my son for the first time in my life. Now, I see my special son climbing the ladder of life with confidence and the will to be successful in life. We are always dedicated in raising autism awareness.